*Marjorie Kann Jackson*

# BLESSINGS OF THE
# CHRISTIAN LIFE

---

Stillwater Books
A Division of Sycamore Creek Press
Fort Worth, Texas

*Blessings of The Christian Life*
© Copyright 2013 by Marjorie Kann Jackson

All rights reserved.

Original art work and cover design: Lynn Jackson Talley

This book is also available on Amazon.com as a Kindle eBook. Visit www.amazon.com/ebooks.

Library of Congress Cataloging-in-Publication Data
Jackson, Marjorie Kann.
Blessings of the Christian Life / Marjorie Kann Jackson.
2nd ed.
p. cm.
ISBN-13: 978-1493709595
1. Christian Living/Inspirational

Second edition, Blessings Series Vol. 2, Stillwater Books 2013
Printed in the United States of America

Unless otherwise noted, all scripture verses are taken from THE HOLY BIBLE, NEW INTERNATIONAL VERSION, NIV. ® Copyright © 1973, 1978, 1984, 2011 by Biblica, Inc.™; and from THE NEW INTERNATIONAL VERSION. Copyright © 1988, 1989, 1990, 1991 by Tyndale House Publishers, Inc. Wheaton, Illinois AND Zondervan Publishing House Grand Rapids Michigan. Used by permission. All rights reserved worldwide.

Scripture quotations marked KJV are taken from the *King James Version* of the Bible. Public domain.

Scripture quotations marked RV are taken from the Revised Version.

Scripture quotations marked (Message) are from *The Message*. Copyright © 1993, 1994, 1995, 1996, 2000, 2001, 2002. Used by permission of Nav Press Publishing Group.

In loving memory of

Mary Jo Scheideman
and in honor of her husband, Blaine.

*They provided a place of blessing
where our Thursday Bible Study met
for more than 10 years. When we
stepped over their threshold we knew
that the presence of the Lord was in
that place.*

# Contents

*Introduction*     8
*Invitation*     9

**Lesson 1:** Why Did Jesus Come? Part 1     12
    Prayer: Dying You Set Me Free     31
    Think on These Things     32

**Lesson 2:** Why Did Jesus Come? Part 2     34
    Prayer: Just Come     48
    Think on These Things     49

**Lesson 3:** Why Did Jesus Come? Part 3     52
    Prayer: Who Do You Say I Am?     68
    Think on These Things     69

**Lesson 4**: Finding New Beginnings     73
    Prayer: Live to Your Honor     86
    Think on These Things     87

**Lesson 5:** Have You Decided To Follow Jesus?     90
    Prayer: I Will Follow You     109
    Think on These Things     110

**Lesson 6:** What Is Our Part in the Christian Life? What Is God's Part?     113
    Prayer: I Want You, Lord     129
    Think on These Things     130

**Lesson 7:** Secret Things and Revealed Things     133
    Prayer: Praise, Love and Honor     144
    Think on These Things     145

**Lesson 8:** What Is the Secret of Jehovah?  148
    Prayer: A Song of Victory  160
    Think on These Things  161
**Lesson 9:** Jubilation in Desolation  163
    Prayer: How Majestic Is Your Name  176
    Think on These Things  177
**Lesson 10:** He Never Changes  180
    Prayer: To Your Name Be the Glory  191
    Think on These Things  192

*The Prayer for Spiritual Life*  194
*Acknowledgments*  196
*Notes*  197

# Introduction

When my father, Dr. Herbert E. Kann, retired from 40 years as a Presbyterian minister he gave me the books he valued most. Dr. G. Campbell Morgan authored many of them. That was my introduction to Dr. Morgan's work.

Throughout the first 40 years of the 20th century Dr. Morgan was considered by many to be the greatest Bible expositor of that day. He explained the truths of Scripture as no one else could.

In 1904, he became pastor of Westminster Chapel in London, England. There were many requests that his sermons be made available in printed form. Each week Dr. Morgan chose one of his weekly messages for publication. At the end of the year they were bound under the title *The Westminster Pulpit*. I have ten of those volumes. These lessons draw heavily on that body of work. They loosely follow his outlines and make use of his matchless word studies. I first taught them in Fort Worth, Texas, in 2006-2008.

My life has been greatly enriched by Dr. Morgan's scholarship and by the insight the Holy Spirit gave to him. This is the second volume I have written in an attempt to share these blessings with a new generation of seekers. Volume 1 is *Blessings of The Holy Spirit*. It is available through Amazon.com.

—*Marjorie Kann Jackson*

# *Invitation*

Come now, and open the door to life change! Let your mind and heart slow their pace. Put aside for a little while the responsibilities of everyday, and join me here.

It has long been recognized that in order to live a life that is rich in spirit, we must become aware of the world that exists within ourselves. It is a world that is totally unseen, but every aspect of our outer world is governed by it and is an expression of it. Such inner worlds are built on a person's own truths. They are usually based on what can be seen and heard and touched and felt. They may express family patterns of thinking and responding or preconceived notions or insights. They may be the product of our education. At any rate, over time they faithfully reveal our interpretations of the circumstances and relationships that life confronts us with. Another way to say this is that the life that exists in us is the life that is lived out through us.

For many people, this private world is filled with thoughts that chronically depress and defeat. They desperately seek escape from it; literally unable to bear the ideas that confront them there. Nothing is worse for them than times alone. Silence or solitude is torture. They busy themselves in work or play, in amusements or distractions, or numb or anesthetize themselves with food or drugs.

Some people have found a different way to live. It is in an inner world that is filled with peace and refreshment for soul and spirit; a world in which God Himself is our constant companion. Jesus spoke of this in John 14:23. *Jesus said, "If anyone loves me, he will obey my teaching. My Father will love him, and we will come to him and make our home with him."*

In Romans 12:2, we read these words, *"And do not conform any longer to the pattern of this world, but be trans-*

*formed by the renewing of your mind. Then you will be able to test and approve what God's will is, his good, pleasing and perfect will."* The Living translation of this verse reads, *"Be a new and different person with fresh newness in all you do and think."*

This book includes the following features:

1. SCRIPTURE REFERENCES ARE GIVEN IN THEIR ENTIRETY. Truth has many facets! As we look at it from different perspectives we gain new understanding. Just as a cut diamond reflects beauty in all its glory as it is examined from a number of angles, so the truth of Scripture acquires clarity and brilliance as we look at it from various viewpoints. In this book, we provide you with that opportunity by including many Scripture references in their entirety so that you can experience Scripture commenting and expanding on Scripture.
2. MEMORIZATION. One Bible verse serves as the text for each lesson. It is suggested for memorization, for it encapsulates the primary teaching of that lesson.
3. PRAYER. At the end of each lesson you will find a prayer. These are the words of Prayer Songs that were given to me long ago. You can make them your own, or use them to lead you to the unique prayers of your heart. The Holy Spirit Himself is our teacher, and as we move into interactive study we want to invite His participation.
4. APPLICATION AND PRACTICE. Also at the end of each lesson you will find questions that will help you focus on the main points. They bring you to the heart of the learning process. They help you think through and practice what you are studying. They can be used for individual meditation, and they are easily adaptable for group use. They encourage

exploration and interaction. Also, a small group can serve as a valuable source of support, inspiration, and accountability. You may want to include time to worship together, to share experiences, to pray for one another, and to plan special activities. You will find pleasure in participating together in this journey!
5. PERSONAL JOURNALING. Throughout, you will find space to record your thoughts and insights. This will be a valuable aspect of the study, for it will make it uniquely your own. I suggest you purchase a small notebook to use in conjunction with the text. This will allow you to expand your notes and to collect ideas for meditation. I like to write my journal as a prayer to God. It is a wonderful way to simply talk to Him as to your very best friend.

May this book help you gain new insight into the blessings of the Christian life. May you discover that it takes you to life that is lived on a higher plane.

To God be the glory!

# Lesson 1
## Why Did Jesus Come?
## Part 1

TEXT: *"The reason the Son of God appeared, was to destroy the devil's work."*

**I John 3:8, NIV**

Why did Jesus come? It stands to reason that if Jesus had never come, the blessings of the Christian life would never have been possible for us. Aside from the revelation of Holy Scripture, I'm sure mankind could not imagine why this One would empty Himself of His prerogatives as Almighty God and leave the glories of heaven to invade the sphere in which we exist. We read of this in Philippians 2:6-8:

> *"Christ Jesus, being in very nature God, did not consider equality with God something to be grasped, but made himself nothing, taking the very nature of a servant, being made in human likeness. And being found in appearance as a man, he humbled himself and became obedient to death — even death on a cross!"*

It is important to understand that Jesus came as a servant of God. Never is He the servant of men.

We can hardly overstate the importance of this subject. Surely the message of the Bible places the coming of Jesus at the very center of God's dealings with us. Throughout the Old Testament everything was pointing toward this great event. The stories of the Old Testament were fulfilled and explained when Jesus came. The prophets and the psalmists of old spoke and sang of His coming; and, once He had come, all of human history proceeded forth from that event, even to this day! The last book of the Bible brings to us the grand finale of human history, and the grand revelation of Jesus Christ. The title of that book should be, *"The Revelation of Jesus Christ"*, for in truth, that is what it is!

Our attention is arrested, not only by the messages that we find bound up for us in the Bible, but by the results that have issued from them throughout the history of mankind. We know that historically, Jesus is without question the most important man who ever lived. In and of itself that is astounding, for He lived as a man of meager means. He was born into a humble family. He had no formal education. He had no financial backing. For the most part, the influential people of his day were against Him from the beginning. They began to plot his death early on, and eventually executed Him as a common criminal. His public ministry lasted for only three and a half years, yet here we are over 2,000 years later and we can observe results that can be traced back to the coming of Christ. So, it is of utmost importance that we understand the purposes of God in the coming of Jesus. Why did He come?

We find part of our answer in the text for this lesson. He came to destroy the works of Satan. That brings us to another question. Why did Satan come to planet earth? What was his purpose in coming? To find our answer we will need to go back, way back to the beginning. It is a fascinating story, and we get our introduction to it in Genesis 1:1 which states, *"In the beginning God created the heavens and the earth."* When was the universe created? That is an answer that has been sought and debated for centuries! Scripture does not give us information for determining how long ago that occurred. However, there is widespread agreement that Genesis 1:1 refers to God's work of original creation. *"In the beginning"* doesn't mean from all eternity. Eternity has no beginning. The Hebrew word used here means in the beginning when there was a beginning. It means in the beginning of the universe as it was subject to time.

Next, we come to Genesis 1:2. *"Now the earth **was** formless and empty, darkness was over the surface of the deep, and the Spirit of God was hovering over the waters."* This brings up yet another question. Did God create the earth as a formless, empty, dark planet? The Hebrew word that we find translated here as *"was"* appears only two other places in the Bible. In both of those places it is translated *"became"*. Some Hebrew scholars say that this could be accurately translated, *"The earth became wrecked and ruined."*

This has led to two interpretations of these verses. The first is known as the Original Chaos Interpretation. It accepts these words as the description of formless matter that existed in the first stage of the creation of the universe. However, there is another interpretation. It is known as The Divine Judgment interpretation. It sees the earth as having been created as perfection. After an unknown length of time that could incorporate millions of years, and most probably in connection with Satan's sin of rebellion against God, judgment fell on the earth; and it became formless and empty and dark. The Divine judgment interpretation points out that these words are a description of the earth only, and not of the universe as a whole. It seems to describe the earth, not as it was originally, but in a state of ruin. Genesis 1:2 tells us, *"Now the earth became formless and empty."*

I am including for you some of the verses that point in the direction of a perfect creation. Here, in Job 38:4-7, God speaks to Job:

> *"Where were you when I laid the earth's foundation? Tell me, if you understand. Who marked off its dimensions? Surely you*

*know! Who stretched a measuring line across it? On what were its footings set, or who laid its cornerstone – while the morning stars sang together and all the angels shouted for joy?"*
In Isaiah 45:18 we read:
*"For this is what the Lord says – he who created the heavens, he is God: he who fashioned and made the earth, he founded it; he did not create it to be empty, but formed it to be inhabited – he says: 'I am the Lord, and there is no other.'"*

In Genesis 1:1, I find the story of a beautiful creation and of a perfect world. Why did God create it? In Colossians 1:16 we read:
*"For by him all things were created: things in heaven and on earth, visible and invisible, whether thrones or powers or rulers or authorities; all things were created by him and for him."*

Why would God create a world that would be ruined? Scripture is the story of God's Love. In 1 John 4:8 and 4:16 we are told that *"God is love"*. Perhaps His Love sought a way to express itself. You may have heard a well-known saying, "Twas great to speak a world from naught, Twas greater to redeem."

Why would judgment fall on planet earth because of Satan's rebellion? In answering that question, we find that there is another story of creation that we must take into account. It is found in Ezekiel 28:11-15. This story is about the creation of Satan, and describes him as he existed before his fall. He was created as the mightiest of the angels, and the Bible says more about him than about all the other angels combined.

*"The word of the Lord came to me (Ezekiel) 'Son of man, take up a lament*

*concerning the king of Tyre and say to him: "'This is what the Sovereign Lord says: 'You were the model of perfection, full of wisdom and perfect in beauty. You were in Eden, the garden of God; every precious stone adorned you: ruby, topaz and emerald, chrysolite, onyx and jasper, sapphire, turquoise and beryl. Your setting and mountings were made of gold;* **on the day you were created** *they were prepared. You were anointed as a guardian cherub, for so I ordained you. You were on the holy mount of God; you walked among the fiery stones. You were blameless in your ways from the day you were created till wickedness was found in you.'"*

Now to verse 17: *"Your heart became proud on account of your beauty, and you corrupted your wisdom because of your splendor."* Here we are pointed beyond the King of Tyre to Satan, who stood as the unseen ruler. I love one of my Dad's notes. He wrote, "God created an angel. That angel made of himself a devil!"

Under God Satan ruled as a mighty angel prince, a guardian cherub, part of the inner circle of angels who had closest access to God. His position in heaven offered him contact with many elements of God's creation. It seems that his rule included the earth in its magnificent, original state, as well as heavenly places. Note that our Ezekiel passage placed him "in Eden, the garden of God". We know he was in the Garden of Eden with Eve. However, some scholars understand this reference to refer to a primal Eden, and it has also been interpreted as referring to heaven itself. At any rate, it points to access that would not be available to an earthly king.

Isaiah 14:12-14 marks the beginning of sin in the universe, and Satan's fall. His sin was his determination to act in independence of the Creator. Here we encounter Satan's statements marked by *"I will!"* Let it be noted that herein lies the heart of all sin. It is the setting of our will against the will of Almighty God.

> *"How you have fallen from heaven, O morning star, son of the dawn!* [In some translations this reads, *"O Lucifer, son of the morning.*] *You have been cast down to the earth, you who once laid low the nations! You said in your heart,* **I will** *ascend to heaven; I* **will** *raise my throne above the stars of God; I* **will** *sit enthroned on the mount of assembly, on the utmost heights of the sacred mountain. I* **will** *ascend above the tops of the clouds; I* **will** *make myself like the Most High."*

Created as an angel of light, as a beautiful and perfect being and as a being with a free moral will, he set his purpose to be like God. He wanted to be God!

We pick up God's judgment of him in Isaiah 14:15-17.

> *"But you are brought down to the grave, to the depths of the pit. Those who see you stare at you, they ponder your fate: 'Is this the man who shook the earth and made kingdoms tremble, the man who made the world a desert, who overthrew its cities and would not let his captives go home?"*

In Jeremiah 4:23-28, we find God's judgment recounted as a cosmic catastrophe. Note how it draws on the imagery of Genesis 1 as it describes the undoing of creation. These are the words of the Lord!

> *"I looked at the earth, and it was formless and empty; and at the heavens, and their light was gone. I looked at the mountains, and they were quaking; all the hills were swaying. I looked, and there were no people;*

> *every bird in the sky had flown away. I looked, and the fruitful land was a desert; all its towns lay in ruins before the Lord, before his fierce anger. This is what the Lord says: 'The whole land will be ruined, though I will not destroy it completely. Therefore, the earth will mourn and the heavens above grow dark, because I have spoken and will not relent, I have decided and will not turn back.'"*

These words also serve in their context to describe God's judgment that was coming against the people of Judah, but the language takes us beyond that to the judgment that fell on that first creation.

Looking back to Genesis, I understand the account there to be of the re-creation of the earth. This interpretation fits in well with the story of this earth as it is written in our geology. It accounts for the eons of time that are part of the history of our planet.

Why did Satan come to the re-created planet earth? His avowed purpose was to reclaim authority over this planet and the world of men. Satan came to reclaim what he saw as his.

Satan had taken it upon himself to oppose God's plan and to purpose for himself and for mankind a way of life that directly opposes the revealed will of God. It is based on a lie. The lie is that we do not need God because we can be like God.

We read how Satan presented this proposition to Eve in Genesis 3:1-4.

> *"Now the serpent was more crafty than any of the wild animals the Lord God had made. He said to the woman, "Did God really say, 'You must not eat from any tree in the garden?'"*

> *The woman said to the serpent, "We may eat fruit from the trees in the garden, but God did say, 'You must not eat fruit from the tree that is in the middle of the garden, and you must not touch it, or you will die.'"*
>
> *"You will not certainly die," the serpent said to the woman."*

It is important to note that neither God nor Satan will impose their will on us. Adam and Eve had a choice, as we do.

Also, worth noting is that we are never tempted to do evil. The temptation is always to change our viewpoint, our perspective, our way of thinking, our paradigm. The temptation is to choose our way over God's way.

He set out to accomplish that through the deception of Eve and the following transgression of both Adam and Eve. Through them he secured the downfall of mankind and the entrance of sin into the world of men. Thus, began Satan's long warfare against the work of God in the interest of humanity. He is the prince of a vast world system that rests upon force, greed, selfishness, sinful pleasure and personal ambition. It enthrones self, and dethrones God. It operates independently of God. We love to sing that this is our Father's world, but in truth Satan holds it in his hands.

This truth is confirmed, in Matthew 4:8-10. These verses tell something of the temptation of Jesus.

> *"Again, the devil took him to a very high mountain and showed him all the kingdoms of the world and their splendor. 'All this I will give you,' he said, 'if you will bow down and worship me.'"*

You see, the kingdoms of the world were and are his to give!

How can this be? Why would God allow it? God puts the propositions Satan proposes to an experimental test. We see a graphic example of this in the story of Job. We also see it in all past history. Dr. Lewis Sperry Chafer wrote in *Systematic Theology1, Vol. II*, that Satan is allowed, and perhaps required to put his scheme of independent action to an experimental test. As it runs its course it will become the ground of its own complete and universal condemnation. It will be a demonstration that will not leave room for one voice to be raised, even Satan's, to claim that his lie could have been proven to be the truth had it been allowed to fully demonstrate itself.

Today this is playing out. Light is pitted against darkness and Truth against falsehood, but the day is coming when the promise of Philippians 2:9-11 will be fulfilled:

> *"Therefore, God exalted him (Jesus) to the highest place and gave him the name that is above every name, that at the name of Jesus every knee should bow, in heaven and on earth and under the earth, and every tongue confess that Jesus Christ is Lord, to the glory of God the Father."*

Given this background, let us go back to our question of why Jesus came. He is the only One who can destroy the works of the devil! Those who lived in the days of Jesus saw Him as a true reformer. He was a soul in conflict with everything that was contrary to the purposes of God. When we say that, there is a sense in which we have stated the whole meaning of His coming.

Our grandchildren are almost grown now. When they were young they would often spend the night with us. It was my joy to tuck them into bed, and to say prayers with them. Most often I would end my prayer by asking God to help them love what He loves, and hate what He hates. Those words explain this characteristic of Jesus. May it be the desire of our hearts.

Let's read I John 3:1-10 in order to see our text within its context:

> *"How great is the love the Father has lavished on us, that we should be called children of God! And that is what we are. The reason the world does not know us is that it did not know him. Dear friends, now we are children of God, and what we will be has not yet been made known. But we know that when he appears, we shall be like him, for we shall see him as he is. Everyone who has this hope in him purifies himself, just as he is pure.*
>
> *Everyone who sins breaks the law; in fact, sin is lawlessness. But you know that he appeared so that he might take away our sins. And in him is no sin. No one who lives in him keeps on sinning. No one who continues to sin has either seen him or known him. Dear children, do not let anyone lead you astray. He who does what is right is righteous, just as he is righteous. He who does what is sinful is of the devil, because the devil has been sinning from the beginning.* **The reason the Son of God appeared was to destroy the devil's work.** *No one who is born of God will continue to sin, because God's seed remains in him; he cannot go on sinning, because he has been born of God. This is how we know who the children of God are and who the children of the devil are; anyone who does not do what is right is not a child of God; nor is anyone who does not love his brother."*

For a long time these verses were confusing to me. What did they mean? How could it be that those who are born of God will not continue to sin? It was just beyond me!

I have come to understand that a natural law and a spiritual law is that the life that is within is the life that will be expressed and lived out through us. I can't plant pansies and get roses! My dog will not give birth to a cat. If the life of Christ is in me, the life of Satan will not be expressed through me.

One of the great blessings of the Christian life is that when we are born again we receive a new nature. It is a nature that does not want to continue in sin. It is a nature that does not want to practice sin. It is a nature that pursues righteousness. As we learn to live out of our spirit as it is indwelt and controlled by the Holy Spirit our lives become demonstrations of Christ living in and through us!

Now, it is interesting to notice the way John describes the coming of Jesus. He doesn't say, *"The reason the Son of God **was born**"*; He says, *"The reason the Son of God **appeared**"*. Some of the translations use the phrase *"**was manifested**"*. This is a word that presupposes a prior existence. In Jesus, this man of Nazareth, One who existed from eternities past was revealed to mankind. In no sense was the incarnation an act by which God began to be. It was not an act whereby God came near to human life. His presence was always with us; but through the miracle of the incarnation He revealed His presence. This enabled Him to do things in human life and human history that could not have been done in any other way.

These words take us back to John's words at the beginning of his epistle.

*"In the beginning"* (the Hebrew meaning here means "in the beginning before there were any beginnings"; in the beginning in eternity past) *was The Word, and The Word was with God, and The Word was God. He was with God in the beginning. Through him all things were made; without*

*him nothing was made that has been made. In him was life, and that life was the light of men. The light shines in the darkness, but the darkness has not understood it.*

*There came a man who was sent from God; his name was John. He came as a witness to testify concerning that light, so that through him all men might believe. He himself was not the light; he came only as a witness to the light. The true light that gives light to every man was coming into the world.*

*He was in the world, and though the world was made through him, the world did not recognize him. He came to that which was his own, but his own did not receive him. Yet to all who received him, to those who believed in his name, he gave the right to become children of God – children born not of natural descent, nor of human decision or a husband's will, but born of God.* **And the Word became flesh** *and made his dwelling among us. We have seen his glory, the glory of the One and Only, who came from the Father, full of grace and truth"* (John 1:1-14).

Then John writes these astounding words in 1 John 1:1: *"That which was from the beginning, which we have heard, which we have seen with our eyes, which we have looked at and our hands have touched — this we proclaim concerning the Word of life."*

These are not exclusively spiritual statements. John was very carefully defining this person; this man, Jesus. He was writing for those who were yet to be born. He was writing for those of us who would not see Him and touch Him. He was saying, "We saw Him! We touched Him!" In all of John's writings his eyes are fixed upon the man, Jesus.

Sometimes in his writings John does not even name Jesus. As we have seen, John wrote, *"THAT which we have seen, THAT which we beheld"*. On another occasion John wrote, *"He that says He abides in Him, ought also to walk even as THAT ONE walked"* (I John 2:6). In these writings, there is no question as to whom John was referring. He was referring to THE SON OF GOD. And how John loved Him! In the story of the Life of Jesus there is no more tender note than the note of John's love for Jesus. It was pure human affection. Each of the disciples loved Him in their own way, but none of them connected with His human personality in such a warm and tender way as did John.

    A long time ago I wondered why Jesus wanted our love. How was it that our love could be sought and valued by the God of all creation? One day, I found my answer. It came to me that every human being loves in a way that is solely their own. I believe that our love is as unique as our fingerprints. I cannot love as you do. You cannot love as I do, and that is why I think our love is deeply valued by God. We all have a one-of-a-kind love to offer Him!

    It was John who laid his head on Jesus bosom. It was John who heard the beating of His heart. It was John who put his own hand on Jesus the Christ; and it was John who knew that underneath the warmth of His human flesh there existed the majesty of Deity.

    *"That which our hands handled, concerning the Word of life."* Pay attention to the contradiction here. Pay attention to the inconsistency. Can we handle words? Can we handle life? Yet John tells us that this is what they did, for he is deeply conscious of *"the Word made flesh"*. He is deeply conscious that He lived among us! He remembers His warmth and His gentleness. He remembers the love in His eyes, and He remembers that He is the Son of God.

    Next, we have our STATEMENT OF PURPOSE. There are things that are to be destroyed. There is a person who is referred to; the devil. Jesus came to destroy the works of the devil. There is an enemy of God, the devil; and Jesus came to destroy his works.

What are his works? Jesus spoke to this in John 8:44. Here, He was speaking to the Pharisees:

*"You belong to your father, the devil, and you want to carry out your father's desire. He was a murderer from the beginning, not holding to the truth, for there is no truth in him. When he lies, he speaks his native language, for he is a liar and the father of lies."*

As a murderer, he destroys life on every level. The Greek word translated *"murderer"* could more forcefully be translated *"man-slayer"*. He would rob mankind of life in all its forms. He destroys life on the highest level in that he destroys spiritual life; and in that process, he alienates mankind from God. He also destroys life on the mental level. Intellectual pursuits that fail to include God lead down paths of darkness because they are rooted in rational blindness. On the physical plane, sin destroys the human body. All of these things lie within the realm of his work as a murderer. He brings destruction to human lives. But he does more than that. He is a liar. In John 8:44, Jesus identifies the devil as "the father of all lies". Where there is no truth there is no light. Despair and ignorance are due to a lack of spiritual light.

In contrast, Jesus of Nazareth is the light of the world! Those who knew Him personally saw that He was completely free of all ignorance. His thinking processes were perfectly clear. He was able to see into the heart of any matter. In John 7, we find Jesus in Jerusalem at the Feast of the Tabernacles. We can pick up the story in John 7:14:

*"Not until halfway through the Feast did Jesus go up to the temple courts and begin to teach. The Jews were amazed and asked,*

> *'How did this man get such learning without having studied?'  Jesus answered, 'My teaching is not my own. It comes from him who sent me. If anyone chooses to do God's will, he will find out whether my teaching comes from God or whether I speak on my own.'"*

This is what the men of education and learning and leadership had to say of Him. "How does this man know, having never learned? How does He know, having never been to school? How can this Man be familiar with the things we studied long and hard to understand? How can He be teaching these things?" They marveled at Him, for here was a man who had never been taught, but who knew. Here was a man who had never learned, but who had all knowledge. It is true to state that all ignorance is the result of our vision of God being clouded. 1 Corinthians 13:12 tells us that we see everything *"as through a glass, darkly"*. It is in proportion to our knowledge of God that we gain clarity of vision. Jesus possessed total clarity.

Jesus is infallible in every way. He is exempt from error. He is absolutely trustworthy. He knows all the laws of the universe; those discovered and those yet to be discovered. He knows all about the spiritual laws that exist, and the laws of science and of medicine and of physics and mathematics. He is definitely not spiritually infallible and scientifically ignorant! There is no limitation in Him. Men were not yet ready for complete knowledge, nor are they today. He said that He had many things to say, but that mankind was not ready to bear them (John 16:12).

On the great day of His second Advent, Christ's great redemptive work will be perfected in humanity. Mankind will be fully restored to God. I believe when that day comes we will laugh to remember that we thought we understood this world. We have barely scratched the surface of the mysteries that surround us. But in that day, we will find ignorance banished forever, and we will discover that we are living in Light! As for today, the liar has brought darkness, and with the darkness has come ignorance and despair.

Satan is also the supreme sinner. Lawlessness is sin, and lawlessness does not mean being without law. It means breaking the law. It means being against the law. All wrong is the work of the devil. All of the wrong done to God, all of the wrong done by man to man, all wrong done by man to himself, all wrong is Satan's work. He violates the law of Love. Cruelty, jealousy, greed, betrayal, deceit, all are works of the devil.

The Son of God was revealed that He might destroy the works of the devil. We saw Jesus at the beginning of our meditation as a soul in conflict with all these things. That indicated His program and prophesied His purpose. At Christmas time, we do not celebrate simply the birth of a little child that one day would give His life a ransom for many. We celebrate the one happening in the course of human events through which God Himself can destroy the works of the devil.

What of this word, *"destroy"*? It means to dissolve and to loosen. This is an English translation of a Greek word that means to be broken to pieces. What has been whole is dissolved, loosened, wrecked and scattered. We must understand the word *"destroyed"*. Jesus was manifested in order to do a work in human history. The result of His work would be that the works of the devil would be loosened and dissolved, wrecked and scattered. What appears even to this day to be cohesive and whole will be separated and dispersed. Jesus came to destroy hatred with love. He came to destroy lawlessness with law. He came to destroy all that ruins and spoils. He came to lift us up, and He came to transform our lives.

In 2 Corinthians 3 verses 17-18 we read of this transformation:

*"Now the Lord is the Spirit, and where the Spirit of the Lord is, there is freedom. And we, who with unveiled faces all reflect the Lord's glory, are being transformed into his likeness with ever-increasing glory, which comes from the Lord, who is the Spirit."*

The Greek word that is translated *"transformed"* holds within it the meaning of being metamorphosed, completely changed, made over in the sense of reversal.

How does that work? Jesus overcomes death with Life. First and foremost, He offers spiritual life, fellowship with God. He offers mental life. We still see through a glass darkly, but more is revealed to us every day. Gradually we begin to hear the singing. From the simplest among us to the most learned, gradually we begin to hear the song. Huxley said that if our ears were more acute we could hear the flowers grow. Morning by morning we open the curtains of our homes and looking out over our gardens or into the softness of sunrise we whisper to ourselves, "Is not God beautiful?" Carlyle called that "the great significance shining through".

Elizabeth Barrett Browning wrote:

Earth's crammed with heaven,
And every common bush afire with God;
But only he who sees, takes off his shoes —
The rest sit round it and pluck blackberries.

Am I one of "the rest"? Are you one of "the rest"? Those who see have received intellectual vision that is part of the God-given gift of Life. The gift of Life was bestowed on us in order to destroy death. Once I have received it, I can laugh death in the face! 1 Corinthians 15:55 says,

*"Where, O death, is your victory? Where, O death, is your sting?"* There is laughter here! Once we trembled before death. Now, we can laugh in his face! Jesus came to destroy the works of the devil by giving us the gift of Life that destroys death. *"Now this is eternal life: that they may know you, the only true God, and Jesus Christ whom you have sent"* (John 17:3).

For the darkness, Jesus came to bring the gift of light, and light always comes out of Life. There is no vision in death. There is no light where there is no life. Knowledge and hope and guidance come with the gift of light. By bringing light into human life Jesus brings light into the world, and thereby destroys the works of the devil.

Light illumines life, but it is the gift of love that brings warmth to life. When we receive God's gift of love, His gift of benevolence and good will, we bring to our world kindness and well wishes and we do small things out of pure love. How is hatred and jealousy and selfishness and greed destroyed? It is destroyed as we, who have received God's gift of love, shed it abroad. In this way, God is destroying the works of the devil.

What about lawlessness? Jesus destroys it by the gift of His law, by the passion He gives us for the rights of God, and by showing us how to find perfect freedom through becoming a bond slave of Jesus Christ.

What are the works of the devil? They are death working within us; a spirit that smothers light and truth by presenting lies to us. They are the darkness that ignorance brings. They are the spirit of hatred and greed and spite and jealousy. They are lawlessness and the refusal to submit to God. They are all things that are unlike God.

The Son of God entered the stream of human history 21 centuries ago. He has transformed the lives of millions of people by destroying the works of the devil. He has given them life more abundantly. He has turned their darkness into light. He has turned selfishness into love, joy, peace, patience, long suffering, kindness and goodness (Galatians 5:22). He has taken lawless people and made them willing and joyful bond servants of Jesus Christ. In these ways, He has destroyed the works of the devil.

And what of the historical meaning of His coming? When Jesus came the scepter was snatched from the usurper. Forces entered human history that dissolved the works of the devil, scattering them and causing them to fail. Yet still today we see all around us the works of the devil manifest. At the same time, we see the fruit of the Spirit of life, and its ultimate victory is certain. God's present relationship to the world lies in the sovereignty of His permission and restraint and His purpose to save out of it an elect people for His heavenly glory.

On a personal level, let me tell you that my victory is not perfectly won. My Master's work is not fully accomplished, but I bear witness to the forces of Jesus Christ that are operating today in me to loosen and destroy and to establish and build up. He came to destroy the works of the devil, and to bring me Life, and Life more abundant. In John 10:10, Jesus said, *"The thief comes only to steal and kill and destroy; I have come that they may have life, and have it to the full."* All of this He accomplishes when He gives us the gift that encompasses all of the other gifts; He gives us the gift of Himself. In John 10:11, Jesus went on to say, *"I am the good shepherd. The good shepherd lays down his life for the sheep."*

May we hold in our hearts a clearer picture of all that Jesus has done and is doing for mankind collectively and for us individually in His coming to destroy the works of the devil. May God grant us thankful and responsive hearts as we accept His unspeakable gift, and reach out in Jesus name to share it with others.

## *Dying You Set Me Free*

Dying You set me free, my Lord.
Dying You set me free.
You give me a new life to live,
It's Your life lived out through me.

I sing Your freedom.
I sing Your Love.
I sing Your wonder and grace;
For You, my Lord, left Your home above,
So I could know You face to face.

## *Think on These Things*

In what sense did the disciples and those of His time see Jesus as a true reformer?




Explain the meaning of the word *"manifested"* or of the word *"appeared"* as if refers to Jesus.




Why do you think God Almighty values your love?

Can you summarize the works of the devil, and how they define his personality?




Has your understanding of Jesus as the Light of the world been broadened by this lesson? Explain your answer.




What is lawlessness?




Explain your understanding of the transformation that God offers to bring to your life.




I think you will enjoy reading and thinking about Hebrews Chapter 2.

## Lesson 2
### Why Did Jesus Come?
### Part 2

TEXT: *"You know that he appeared so that he might take away our sins. And in Him is no sin."*

**I John 3:5, NIV**

Our last lesson had as its text I John 3:8. *"The reason the Son of God appeared was to destroy the devil's work."* This week our text is I John 3:5. *"You know that He appeared so that he might take away our sins. And in Him is no sin."*

In review, we want to remember that our last lesson was on how Jesus came to destroy the works of the devil. We defined those works as being death, darkness, hatred, and lawlessness. However, it can correctly be said that one word expresses all the works of the devil. It is the word sin.

*"Sin"* is a word that we hear very little of these days. For one thing, it is a politically incorrect word. We have discovered words to use that are much less painful, and at the same time are much less accurate. We use words like mistakes, and bad choices and poor decisions. It is even said that all people have the right to determine for themselves what is right and what is wrong, making values relative and ruling out sin completely. No, we don't hear the word *"sin"* much anymore.

However, God does not shy away from using that word. Dr. C.I. Scofield, perhaps best known for his notes that appear in the *Scofield Reference Bible*, defines the literal meanings of the Hebrew and Greek words that are translated into English as *"sin"* and *"sinner"*. SIN is TRANSGRESSION in that it is the overstepping of the divine boundary that God has set between good and evil. Psalm 51 was written by David as a prayer that God would forgive his transgression. It was written after he had committed adultery with Bathsheba. Here we will look at verse 1. *"Have mercy on me, O God, according to your unfailing love; according to your great compassion blot out my transgressions."*

Sin is also INIQUITY; a wicked act; an act that is inherently wrong. Romans 1:28-32 speaks of this:

> *"Furthermore, since they did not think it worthwhile to retain the knowledge of God, he gave them over to a depraved mind, to do what ought not to be done. They have become filled with every kind of wickedness, evil, greed and depravity. They are full of envy, murder, strife, deceit and malice. They are gossips, slanderers, God-haters, insolent, arrogant and boastful; they invent ways of doing evil; they disobey their parents; they are senseless, faithless, heartless, ruthless. Although they know God's righteous decree that those who do such things deserve death, they not only continue to do these very things but also approve of those who practice them."*

Sin is ERROR. It is believing something that is untrue or moving away from what is right. Romans 1:18 states, *"The wrath of God is being revealed from heaven against all the godlessness and wickedness of men who suppress the truth by their wickedness."*

Sin is FAILURE to meet God's Divine Standard. It is falling short of His mark. Romans 3:23 tells us, *"For all have sinned and fall short of the glory of God."*

Sin is TRESPASSING. It is intruding with self-will into the arena of divine authority.

> *"As for you, you were dead in your transgressions and sins in which you used to live when you followed the ways of this world*

*and of the ruler of the kingdom of the air, the spirit who is now at work in those who are disobedient. All of us also lived among them at one time, gratifying the cravings of our sinful nature and following its desires and thoughts. Like the rest, we were by nature objects of wrath"* (Ephesians 2:1-2).

Sin is LAWLESSNESS. It is chaos and disorder and confusion brought about by a lack of control. It is spiritual anarchy. In I Timothy 1:8-11 Paul writes:

*"We know that the law is good if one uses it properly. We also know that the law is made not for the righteous but for lawbreakers and rebels, the ungodly and sinful, the unholy and irreligious; for those who kill their fathers or mothers, for murderers, for adulterers and perverts, for slave traders and liars and perjurers – and for whatever else is contrary to the sound doctrine that conforms to the glorious gospel of the blessed God, which he entrusted to me."*

Finally, sin is UNBELIEF, which is an insult to the personal truthfulness of God. In John 16:8-9 we see, *"When he (the Holy Spirit) comes, he will convict the world of guilt in regard to sin and righteousness and judgment: in regard to sin, because men do not believe in me."*

Where did sin come from? It originated with Satan. Sin entered the world through Adam, and it is universal with the exception of Jesus Christ. It is important to understand that we are not sinners because we sin. We sin because we are born sinners. We are all born with spirits that are separated from God; spiritually dead to Him. This is the inheritance of mankind through Adam. This is why Jesus Christ offers us a new birth.

> *"Wherefore, as by one man sin entered into the world, and death by sin, and so death passed upon all men, for all have sinned."*
> (Romans 5:12).
>
> *"For just as through the disobedience of the one man, the many were made sinners, so also through the obedience of the one man, the many will be made righteous"* (Romans 5:19).

The penalty for sin is both physical and spiritual death. Death is not extinction. It is separation. Physical death is the separation of the soul and spirit from the body. Spiritual death is separation of the soul and spirit from God. *"For the wages of sin is death, but the gift of God is eternal life in Christ Jesus our Lord"* (Romans 6:23).

There is no remedy for sin aside from the sacrificial death of Jesus, so His reason for coming to earth was simple. He came to meet our deepest and most pressing need. He appeared so that He might take away our sins. In the economy of God, under His divine plan, there was only one way that purpose could be accomplished. That would be through the coming of Jesus.

Our thinking is overwhelmed as we try to grasp the magnitude of it, and we find that our thoughts stop short at our own sins. Sins; all that stands between God and man, and all that stands between us and others. Sins; all that makes us afraid of God and afraid of one another. Sins; the missing of the mark, the falling short, whether willfully or out of ignorance. Sins; all of the thoughts and words and deeds that have failed to measure up to God's Divine purpose and ideal.

This is what John the Baptist meant when, looking upon Jesus, he said, *"Behold the Lamb of God, which taketh away the sin of the world"* (John 1:29, KJV). John used the same word here, but in the singular; *"sin"*. Here John is referring to the principle of a wrong life that reveals itself in lawless acts.

Now, let us turn our attention to the phrase, *"to take away"*. Watch closely here, because this statement does not declare a process. It is not describing a work in progress. It is a statement of the result.

The Hebrew meaning of these words is illustrated in the story we find in Leviticus 16. Each year on the Day of Atonement two goats were presented to the High Priest. One was for the Lord, and was sacrificed as a sin offering. The other goat was the scapegoat. The High Priest would place his hands on the head of the scapegoat. He would confess over it all the sins of the Israelites, and then the goat would be driven far away, out into the wilderness, *"into a solitary place"* Leviticus 16:22 tells us. From there it would be released into the desert.

This represented the two ways in which God was dealing with the sin of the Israelites. It was forgiven through the sacrifice of the first goat. Then, their guilt was removed. The symbolism was that the sins would be lifted from one and placed upon the other. The sin was forgiven, and the guilt was to be carried away, out of consciousness and out of experience never to return.

*"He appeared so that he might take away our sins."* The Greek word translated *"take away"* has also been translated, *"bear"*. If we take this word back to its root meaning it means *"to lift"*. Jesus was manifested to lift sins. He was manifested so that He could come into the lives of human beings and be in a relationship with them in which He could come under the load of sin that weighed so heavily upon them and lift the sins up and take them upon Himself. He would pay the penalty sin imposes. Romans 6:23 tells us that *"The wages of sin is death, but the gift of God is eternal life in Christ Jesus our Lord."* God does not offer

us cheap forgiveness. Sin is forgiven because the debt was paid.

This old hymn expresses it so well:

> Jesus paid it all. All to Him I owe.
> Sin had left a crimson stain.
> He washed it white as snow.

Not only would sins be forgiven. He would take them far away. Psalm 103:12 tells us that *"As far as the east is from the west, so far has He removed our transgressions from us."* It is important to note that the psalmist does not say, "As far as the north is from the south." When you go north you finally reach a point at which you are no longer going north. You are going south. On the other hand, when you start going west you never stop going west. There is no point at which you start going east. There is no line of demarcation. So far has God removed our transgressions from us!

Think of the things in your life that lurk every day somewhere around the edges of consciousness; the things you did that you wish you had never done or the words you said that you wish you had never said. Oh, if only you could go back to that day, to that hour. If only you could do it over again you would do it differently! But there is no going back. There is no taking that chapter out of your life. We've all learned to live with such things. We've tried to accommodate them. Most of the time we don't think about them, but still they are there, lying just below the level of consciousness. How many times has the wail echoed down through the halls of time; if only. If only! If only!!

There are those who are careless about such matters. They refuse to take them seriously. They rationalize. They excuse themselves. They may say that it was all just part of growing up. It was no big deal. The human heart can be ingenious in the ways it finds to excuse itself.

Then, there are those who are in agony. There are many people who believe that the degree of guilt they feel is a measure of the degree of their spirituality. They understand that God forgives their sins, but they think they must bear the guilt as long as they live. They know their sin, and they loathe it. It lies as a perpetual burden on their souls. There are many people who have never spoken about it to another human being. They have never confessed it, but they hate the memory of it.

To all of us Jesus says, "I have come to lift all sin from you. This is the meaning of my coming. I appeared to pay the price, to lift it up off you, and to carry it far away never to return. I have come to carry it out of your experience. I have come to carry it out of your consciousness. I have come to take your sins away."

These are either the kindest or the cruelest words that were ever spoken. They hold within them the kindness of the heart of God if they are true, and if they are false they are terribly cruel. Can it be that someone, somewhere, somehow entered human history to lift sins and to carry them away? Can it be that by some deep mystery that I will never fully understand One appeared who could get beneath my sins, my impure thoughts, my bitter words, my unholy behavior and could lift them up and carry them away? Oh, how I long for such a One; a Savior who could give me a clean slate and a new beginning.

Our text tells us that this is THE GREAT PURPOSE of the coming of Jesus, and now in order to understand it in a fuller and more powerful way let us turn our attention to the process itself. Last week our text unveiled the purpose of Christ's coming in gaining victory over the one who is the enemy of God and of the human race. I believe that the supreme value of our text this week is that it indicates to us THE PROCESS through which that purpose is being accomplished. *"He appeared to take away sins."*

Without question, the *"He"* referred to is the Son of God. Here we find, as we often do in the writings of John, that he has his eyes fixed on the Man of Nazareth; and yet John looks through Him to God. The One who appeared to lift up our sins is none other than the Son of God. He is the Word made flesh. He is flesh, but He is the Word. John had seen Him. John had touched Him. John had listened to the beating of His heart. John had experienced Him with his senses, and John knew Him as The Word through the revelation of the Holy Spirit.

He appeared. Who was He before He appeared? Whoever He was before He appeared He was in His appearance, and that is who He is in the taking away of sins!

We see here that immediately after John makes the affirmation, *"He appeared to take away sins,"* he adds another phrase. *"In Him is no sin."* This could just as well be translated, "Missing of the mark was not in Him." It was not in Him to fail. It was not in Him to fall short. The One in whom there was no missing of the mark appeared on the scene of history. He was revealed. He was manifested. He appeared for the purpose of lifting up and bearing away and causing not to be, the guilt, the shortcomings and the missing of the mark of others.

We can correctly interpret John's language only as we go back to search His writings. In introduction to the gospel of John he wrote, *"In the beginning was the Word, and the Word was with God, and the Word was God. He was with God in the beginning"* (John 1:1). The Word, (Jesus) never missed the mark. Through all the immeasurable ages He was sinless. Everything that was created sprang from Him. *"Through him all things were made; without him nothing was* made that has been made" (John 1:3). He was the creator and He was the sustainer and He never missed the mark. Later on, *"The Word became flesh and made his dwelling among us. We have seen his glory, the glory of the One and Only who came from the Father, full of grace and truth"* (John 1:14). Still, He never missed the mark. Then we see Him yielding Himself to death:

> *"Later, knowing that all was now completed, and so that the Scripture would be fulfilled, Jesus said, 'I am thirsty.' A jar of wine vinegar was there, so they soaked a sponge in it, put the sponge on a stalk of the hyssop plant, and lifted it to Jesus' lips. When He had received the drink, Jesus said, 'It is finished.' With that, he bowed his head and gave up his spirit"* (John 19:28-30).

Even then He never missed the mark. He rose from the dead, and He sits at the right hand of the Father at the center of God's universe. He is the same person, from the endless ages in which He has always existed, through His life and death and resurrection until today, and He has never missed the mark.

> *"For this reason, ever since I heard about your faith in the Lord Jesus and your love for all the saints, I have not stopped giving thanks for you, remembering you in my prayers. I keep asking that the God of our Lord Jesus Christ, the glorious Father, may give you the Spirit of wisdom and revelation, so that you may know him better. I pray also that the eyes of your heart may be enlightened in order that you may know the hope to which he has called you, the riches of his glorious inheritance in the saints, and his incomparably great power for us who believe.*

> *That power is like the working of his mighty strength, which he exerted in Christ when he raised him from the dead and seated him at his right hand in the heavenly realms, far above all rule and authority, power and dominion, and every title that can be given, not only in the present age but also in the one to come. And God placed all things under his feet and appointed him to be head over everything for the church, which is his body, the fullness of him who fills everything in every way"* (Ephesians 1:15-23).

He appeared, and we are trying to grasp this enormous truth that this One who appeared was indeed the Son of God who could and would bear up our sins. We know that if He was a man, even if He was a perfect man, a sinless man, He would not be able to take away the sins of others. Consider the promise of His birth. *"You are to give him the name Jesus, because he will save His people from their sins"* (Matthew 1:21). And does He save them from hell? Of course, but only by saving them from their sins. The shepherds heard the angels, and what did the angels say? *"Today in the town of David a Savior has been born unto you; he is Christ the Lord"* (Luke 2:11). The promise of Jesus' birth was that He is the One who would appear in human history who could lift sins as our Savior.

For 33 long years, this Person met all the forces of human temptation and overcame them. Those were years in which His sinlessness became visible to mankind. His words revealed the seriousness of sin and the meaning of sin. With His words and with His life He rebuked sin, and called people to turn their backs on it. And what were His miracles, the signs and wonders He performed? Primarily they were works that overcame the results of sin. We have been taught that the miracles of Jesus were supernatural, but if we study them carefully we see that He restored the unnatural to the natural. In curing disease, He restored people to a normal physical condition. He took away the results of sin. In His healing ministry and in bringing people back from the dead, we see Him engaged relentlessly in a battle with the consequences of sin, and time after time demonstrating His power over it.

Now we come to the final thing in His appearance; the process of His death. It is at the cross that we behold the final fulfillment of those words that John the Baptist heralded on the banks of the river Jordan: *"Look, the Lamb of God, who takes away the sin of the world"* (John 1:29, NIV).

We can't interpret these words in the context of the day in which we live. We have to hear them in the light of John's day and time. This was a Hebrew prophet speaking to Hebrew people, and when they heard of a Lamb taking away sins they could not escape thinking of the long line of symbolical sacrifices that they had carried to the temple. They had been taught that by some process that remained shrouded in mystery for them, this sacrifice of the lambs pointed to a way whereby sin could be dealt with. So, it was at the hour of His death that mankind could see as never before the meaning of our text: *"He appeared to take away sins."*

Jesus, being crucified on a garbage heap, and God is responsible? What kind of priest becomes the sacrifice? Priests offer sacrifices. Our Great High Priest was the sacrifice. Christianity stands alone among the religions of this world with such a story to tell. Jesus was not made a sinner for us. He was made sin for us! This is expressed in 2 Corinthians 5:21 where we read, *"God made him who had no sin to be sin for us, so that in him we might become the righteousness of God."* What does that mean? Much about this story lies outside the realm of human understanding, but perhaps the meaning here was fully expressed in the anguish of Jesus' cry from the cross. *"My God, my God, why have you forsaken me?"* Sin is all that separates us from God, and the One who had forever been One with the Father became sin and bore that separation in our behalf. There is no narrative in all of human history like this one!

You see, the One who cannot be measured came. The One who is above all created things; heavens and earth, suns and stars, above the angels and archangels, above all powers and principalities, the One infinitely above them all came to lift off our sins! In amazement, we stand at the cross, realizing that, like everything else in this story, it stands as a manifestation. Things that had been hidden became obvious and apparent. At the cross, eternal things became visible. There, in the presence of sin, love and light became sorrow; and there, in the presence of sin love and light became joy! *It was "for the joy that was set before Him that He endured the cross"* (Hebrews 12:2). The cross stands as the historic revelation, the ultimate revelation, the conclusive appearance of the abiding fact of the Love that lies within the heart of God. One man could never bear the sins of another, much less the sins of the entire human race; but this One Who appeared is God. He alone can gather into His eternal life all mankind. He alone can take all of our sorrow and all of our sin, and lift them off of us.

Let us acknowledge that the facts surrounding His coming are eternal. Jesus Christ was the lamb of God, *"slain before the foundation of the world"* (Revelation 13:8). However, it was through the appearance of those facts in time and in this world that our sins are forgiven. *"He appeared to take away sins."* It required the *"He"*. God's love for us became a dynamic power in human life when it appeared in human form through the living of a perfect life and the dying of a sacrificial death. Because of the cross of Jesus Christ, it is well with my soul.

There are those who say that God being God could have brought this same deliverance without such suffering. The one who would say that knows nothing about sin. Sin and suffering will forever coexist. One cannot exist without the other. The moment there is sin there is suffering, and that suffering is multiplied many times over in the heart of God.

Our free will remains forever a factor to be dealt with. John 3:16-21 lays out clearly the part that it plays:

*"For God so loved the world that he gave his one and only Son, that whosoever believes in him shall not perish but have eternal life. For God did not send his Son into the world to condemn the world, but to save the world through him. Whoever believes in him is not condemned, but whoever does not believe stands condemned already because he has not believed in the name of God's one and only Son. This is the verdict: Light has come into the world, but men loved darkness instead of light because their deeds were evil. Everyone who does evil hates the light, and will not come into the light for fear that his deeds will be exposed. But whoever lives by the truth comes into the light, so that it may be seen plainly that what he has done has been done through God."*

From the beginning our sin caused God great sorrow. Through the incarnation, through the manifestation, through the birth of Jesus the sorrow of the Godhead became fully visible. Punishment and forgiveness, justice and grace met at the cross of Christ, and nothing was compromised. May that truth capture our will. From this day forward may we accept fully the unspeakable gift that He so freely offers us. May we live in the blessed awareness that He has borne our sins. He lifts them off of us. He takes them away from us; take them away that they might never haunt us again.  May we open our lives to fully accept this matchless gift of His mercy and grace.  May we bow before Him in obedience and trust, in adoration and thanksgiving.  To God be the glory!

## *Just Come*

I can come to Him just as I am.

His love reaches where nothing else can.

His grace is abundant,

His life, full and free;

And it's mine to receive,

For He gave His life for me.

# Think on These Things

Have you noticed that we seldom hear the word "sin" these days? Why do you think that is so? Do you think people feel less guilty because of that?




Dr. Scofield points out seven words from scripture that define sin. List those words.




Did God create the devil? Explain your answer and explain where sin came from.

How did sin enter the world, and what is the punishment it imposes on all of mankind?

Can you comment on how it is that we are not sinners because we sin? How is it that we all are sinners?

How did the offering of the two goats by the High Priest on the Day of Atonement illustrate the result of the redemption Jesus Christ offers to us?

Can you list several of the specific points in your life at which you are or have been aware of your need for God's forgiveness?

Can you explain how the forgiveness of our sins destroys the work of the devil? Can you give an illustration of how that plays out in your life?

I once read a book in which the author stated that she would never accept a God who would sacrifice His own son. Can you share your thoughts on this?

Are you able to define the meaning of this lesson to you?

I think you will enjoy reading and thinking about 1 John Chapter 1 and 1 John 2:1-17.

## Lesson 3
### Why Did Jesus Come?
### Part 3

TEXT: *"He that has seen Me has seen the Father."*

***John 14:9, NIV***

In this lesson, we come to our third study on why Jesus came. Our first lesson was on the fact that Jesus came to destroy the works of the devil. Our second lesson was on the fact that Jesus came to take away sins. Now, we will see that he came to show us The Father. Our text is His own statement of this truth. This statement is simple and to the point, yet of all the things Jesus said about His relationship with His Father, none is more comprehensive, exhaustive, inclusive, complete and thorough than this. *"He that has seen Me has seen the Father"* (John 14:9).

Jesus' last hours with His disciples were passing quickly. He was talking to them, and four times they interrupted Him. First, in John 13:36, Peter said, *"Lord, where are You going?"* Then, in John 14:5, while Jesus was answering Peter, *"Thomas said, Lord, we do not know where You are going, so how can we know the way?"* Then, as Jesus was dealing with Thomas, Philip said, *"Lord, show us the Father and that will be enough for us"* (John 14:8). Before Jesus was finished with Philip, Jude questions in John 14:22, *"But Lord, why do you intend to show yourself to us and not to the world?"*

Jesus knew that His own followers did not understand Him. He knew that they expected Him to reveal himself to be The Messiah, and to set up an earthly kingdom. He knew they could not walk the way of the cross with Him. He saw their fear of the unknown, and patiently and gently He worked with them, teaching them and answering their questions and filling their minds with truth.

Philip's interruption came out of his conviction that Jesus had a special relationship with the Father. Philip had been with Jesus long enough to be familiar with His line of thought. He had heard Jesus speak of God as *"My Father"*. Philip knew the history of his people. Philip knew of how their elders had ascended the mountain and how they saw God there. Philip knew that the prophet had declared that *"In the year that King Uzziah died, I saw the Lord."* Philip knew that Ezekiel declared that he had seen God in majesty and glory, and Philip was hoping that God might be revealed to them as He had been revealed to people in the past.

Philip's request was based on his memories of how God had revealed Himself to men of old, and on what little understanding he possessed of Jesus' relationship with His Heavenly Father. *"Could You just show us Your Father?"*, he asked. As for Jesus, He answered Philip in the everyday speech of one friend to another. Looking kindly into his face Jesus answered:

> *"Don't you know me, Philip, even after I have been among you such a long time? Anyone who has seen me has seen the Father. How can you say, 'Show us the Father?' Don't you believe that I am in the Father, and that the Father is in me? The words I say to you are not just my own. Rather, it is the Father, living in me, who is doing his work. Believe me when I say that I am in the Father and the Father is in me; or at least believe on the evidence of the miracles themselves"* (John 14:9-11).

Notice the utter simplicity of these words, and then notice the utter audacity of them! Put those words into the mouth of any other teacher who has ever lived, and you will recognize what a fearless and daring thing that was to say.

Yet, looking into the face of one man who was giving voice to the universal cry of the human spirit, ("Oh, if only we could see God!") who was giving expression to the hunger of the human soul, Jesus answered; *"He who has seen Me has seen the Father."* Jesus was claiming absolute identity with God in this declaration. It was a statement that would mark Him for execution!

As the centuries have passed, His claim has been validated. Mankind's conception of Almighty God came through this One who said, *"He who has seen Me has seen the Father."* Our purpose in this lesson will be to consider what that revelation means to the human race and what it means to individuals.

First, let us consider what conception man had of God before Christ came. If we look at the Hebrew idea of God, we can see that before Jesus came the intellectual knowledge of God had been developing; yet that was accompanied by less and less morality. In studying the Old Testament, we will be struck by the fact that gradually a clearer picture of God had emerged. Men were confronted by the unity of a triune God, by the holiness of God, the might of God, the power of God, the judgment of God and the goodness and love and patience of God. As the ages passed, men had come to see these things.

However, at the same time we cannot read the story of the ancient Hebrew people without seeing that morally speaking they went from bad to worse! Life in Abraham's time was purer than life at the time of the kings of Israel. Life at the time of the kings was purer than the life that the prophets described. It seems that in proportion to the intellectual conception men held of God it seemed more and more unthinkable to them that God could be interested in their lives. Morality mattered less and less because it was not grounded in a personal relationship, an intimate connection, with God. What faith they had was grounded in the intellect, and not in the heart.

In a very real sense that scenario has played over and over again throughout human history. In our day, as our knowledge of science and of the universe has expanded our concept of God has expanded as well. How has that affected us? There are those who declare that God is unknowable. Some declare that God does not exist. There are also many who define Him as a great force or as complete intelligence. The explosion of knowledge that has occurred over the last 100 years has led some to believe that they don't need God. Some, for all practical purposes, see themselves as Gods; but when God is seen in these ways man loses the sense of relationship to Him.

Let us look now at the Gentile conception of God. It has been marked by an underlying conviction or a universal sense that there is a God. However, in spite of that, the moral standard has completely broken down. Occasionally there have been flashes of clear light, but that has been followed by the repeated degradation of religion. Today Christianity is under serious attack from all sides.

When Jesus came, a child was born and angels spoke tidings of great joy. A generation passed quickly; a generation during which that child grew in wisdom and stature and in favor with God and man. A generation passed of teaching and working and gathering a small group of disciples. Then Jesus, standing in the midst of them and at the same time in the midst of all humanity looked into the face of one man and answered the cry of his heart by saying, *"He who has seen Me has seen the Father."*

Centuries have passed since His coming. What did it mean? His coming brought mankind to a new consciousness of God. What did it reveal about Him? First, Jesus' life and His teaching confirmed all of the things about God that men had come to know in ages past. He reemphasized the unity of a triune God. His Life was a demonstration of unity in plurality in that mankind saw what oneness within the Godhead looked like and how it functioned. Also, Jesus declared and demonstrated the might of God in what He did and in what He said. He insisted on the holiness of God in His teaching and in His living, and finally in the mystery of His dying; and He demonstrated for all to see the greatness of God's Love.

But He did far more than that. Over the centuries men had been reaching for more, but somehow, they had never found it. Through Jesus, what had been hidden was finally revealed. Jesus said, *"He that has seen Me, has seen the Father."* Take note here! Not "Jehovah". Not "Adonai". Not "Elohim". Not any of the names of the Old Testament that were suggestive of who God was; but *"The Father"*. It was through Jesus that the fatherhood of God was revealed. Never had such a God been imagined!

What does fatherhood indicate? It is a term of deepest love and tenderness, but it is also a term of discipline and law. Over and above all else fatherhood means that if a child wanders off the father will suffer anything to bring his lost child back home. Within the realm of religion this emerged as an entirely new truth! How could it be that this mighty God, this holy God, this God above all gods could love with such an everlasting Love that He would sacrifice Himself to save His child? Mankind had never known such a God, nor could they imagine such a God!

For centuries men lived in fear of their Gods. In some societies, they sacrificed their own children in their effort to appease their Gods. They deprived themselves. They mutilated themselves. They tried to make themselves worthy of blessing. When Jesus came a different kind of God was revealed. Of all the religions of the world, Christianity is the only one that claims a God who sacrificed

Himself to save us! Just think of it!! Mankind discovered a God of infinite Love who gave His life for them. This was a truth that burst upon the consciousness of the world, sending rivers of cleansing and renewal and regeneration coursing through it.

This was the impact on the world. But what of the impact on individuals? When Jesus Christ first comes into the life of one who has not known Him before, He will fulfill all that lies in that heart and life that is true. He is The Truth! By the same token, He will correct all that is in that mind and heart that is false.

In our world today there exists a great divide between our claim to religion and virtuous conduct. As long as that exists it will be possible for a person to be highly religious and at the same time highly immoral. It is only when people see clearly the heart of God and the sacrifice of God, His unity and might, His holiness and love that they begin to understand, perhaps for the first time, that Christianity means morality. As a true child of God, a person can discern between good and evil and will be drawn to choose what is good.

In thinking of the effect of Jesus' coming on the individual, perhaps we can find no better illustration than we find in Philip. Philip said, *"Could You just show us Your Father?"* Jesus answered with a question of His own. *"Don't you know me, Philip? I have been with you a long time. Do you still not know Me? If you have seen me you have seen the Father."* Surely Jesus meant that Philip had seen enough of Him to have found the Father!

What had Philip seen? What revelations had been given to this man who felt that he had not seen? Jesus was saying that Philip might have seen. To what was Jesus referring? Let's look at what Scripture tells us Philip had seen.

Matthew, Mark and Luke refer to Philip as one of the Apostles. That is all they say about him. All of his story is found in the Book of John. John tells us of four occasions when Philip is seen with Jesus. We will look at the first three and then at the fourth one in which our text occurs.

We quickly discover that Philip was the first man Jesus called to follow Him. He was not the first man to follow Jesus. Two men preceded Philip, and they followed Jesus in response to the teaching of John. In the first chapter of John's gospel it states that *"Jesus found Philip and said to him, 'Follow Me.'"* Philip was the first man to hear *"Follow Me"* from the mouth of Jesus, as we see in John 1:43. According to Philip's own confession, the first thing that he saw in Jesus was that He embodied all of the ideals of Moses and the prophets. *"Philip found Nathanael and told him, 'We have found the one Moses wrote about in the law, and about whom the prophets also wrote – Jesus of Nazareth, the son of Joseph"* (John 1:35). The word Philip used here referred to the whole body of Old Testament teaching. What Philip meant was, "We have found The One that embodies all of the messages of all of the prophets. We have found Him!" Can imagine the excitement? The conviction had taken root in Philip's soul that this was truly the long awaited One!

We next find Philip in John 6. Multitudes had gathered around Jesus, and they were hungry. We will pick up this story in John 6:1-14:

> *"Sometime after this, Jesus crossed to the far shore of the Sea of Galilee (that is, the Sea of Tiberius), and a great crowd of people followed him because they saw the miraculous signs he had performed on the sick. Then Jesus went up on a mountainside and sat down with his disciples. The Jewish Passover Feast was near.*

> *When Jesus looked up and saw a great crowd coming toward him, he said to Philip, 'Where shall we buy bread for these people to eat?' He asked this only to test him, for he already had in mind what he was going to do.*
>
> *Philip answered him, 'Eight months wages would not buy enough bread for each one to have a bite!' Another of his disciples, Andrew, Simon Peter's brother, spoke up, 'Here is a boy with five small barley loaves and two small fish, but how far will they go among so many?'*
>
> *Jesus said, 'Have the people sit down.' There was plenty of grass in that place, and the men sat down, about five thousand of them. Jesus then took the loaves, gave thanks, and distributed to those who were seated as much as they wanted. He did the same with the fish.*
>
> *When they had all had enough to eat, he said to his disciples, 'Gather the pieces that are left over. Let nothing be wasted.' So, they gathered them and filled twelve baskets with the pieces of the five barley loaves left over by those who had eaten.*
>
> *After the people saw the miraculous sign that Jesus did, they began to say, 'Surely this is the Prophet who is to come into the world.' Jesus, knowing that they intended to come and make him king by force, withdrew again to a mountain by himself."*

Let us note how Jesus prayed. He didn't say, "Father we need a miracle, and we are believing You for it right now."

He didn't gather his disciples around him to agree with Him in prayer. He simply gave thanks! He simply said thank You!! He was in agreement with His Father, and He was saying "Thank You. Thank You for Your purposes. Thank You for Your will. Thank You if this food goes around. Thank You if we all leave hungry. I thank You for whatever You have in mind for us. Thank You, Father. Thank You." As you read your Bible, notice how often Jesus' prayers were simply prayers of thanksgiving.

Without a doubt, Philip saw Jesus demonstrate power to supernaturally satisfy physical hunger. But that was not all! Let's read John 6:16-40:

> "When evening came, his disciples went down to the lake, where they got into a boat and set of across the lake for Capernaum. By now it was dark, and Jesus had not yet joined them. A strong wind was blowing and the waters grew rough.
>
> When they had rowed three or three and a half miles, they saw Jesus approaching the boat, walking on the water; and they were terrified. But he said to them 'It is I; don't be afraid.' Then they were willing to take him into the boat, and immediately the boat reached the shore where they were heading.
>
> The next day the crowd that had stayed on the opposite shore of the lake realized that only one boat had been there, and that Jesus had not entered it with his disciples, but that they had gone away alone. Then some boats from Tiberius landed near the place where the people had eaten the bread after the Lord had given thanks. Once the crowd realized that neither Jesus nor his disciples were there, they got into the boats and went to Capernaum in search of Jesus.

*When they found him on the other side of the lake, they asked him, 'Rabbi, when did you get here?' Jesus answered, 'I tell you the truth, you are looking for me, not because you saw miraculous signs but because you ate the loaves and had your fill. Do not work for food that spoils, but for food that endures to eternal life, which the Son of Man will give you. On him God the Father has placed his seal of approval.'*

*Then they asked him, 'What must we do to do the works God requires?' Jesus answered, 'The work of God is this: to believe in the one he has sent.' So they asked him, 'What miraculous sign then will you give that we may see it and believe you? What will you do? Our forefathers ate the manna in the desert; as it is written: 'He gave them bread from heaven to eat.'"*

*Jesus said to them, 'I tell you the truth, it is not Moses who has given you the bread from heaven, but it is my Father who gives you the true bread from heaven. For the bread of God is he who comes down from heaven and gives life to the world.'*

*'Sir' they said, 'from now on give us this bread.'*

*Then Jesus declared, 'I am the bread of life. He who comes to me will never go hungry, and he who believes in me will never be thirsty. But as I told you, you have seen me and still you do not believe. All that the Father gives me will come to me, and whoever comes to me I will never drive away. For I have come down from heaven not to do my will but to do the will of him who sent me. And this is the will of him who sent me, that I shall lose none of all that he has given me, but raise them up at the last day. For my Father's will is that everyone who looks to the Son and believes in him shall have eternal life, and I will raise him up at the last day.'"*

Without a doubt, Philip saw Jesus walk on water. Without a doubt, Philip heard Jesus explaining to the crowd that He was *"the bread of life"*. So, Philip saw Jesus as One who was able to satisfy spiritual hunger as well as physical hunger.

We next see Philip in John 12:20-35:

*"Now there were some Greeks among those who went up to worship at the Feast. They came to Philip, who was from Bethsaida in Galilee, with a request. 'Sir,' they said, 'we would like to see Jesus.' Philip went to tell Andrew; Andrew and Philip in turn told Jesus. Jesus replied, 'The hour has come for the Son of Man to be glorified. I tell you the truth, unless a kernel of wheat falls to the ground and dies, it remains only a single seed. But if it dies, it produces many seeds. The man who loves his life will lose it, while the man who hates his life in this world will keep it for eternal life. Whoever serves me must follow me; and where I am, my servant also will be. My Father will honor the one who serves me.*

*Now my heart is troubled, and what shall I say? 'Father, save me from this hour? No, it was for this reason I came to this hour. Father, glorify your name!' Then a voice came from heaven, 'I have glorified it, and will glorify it again.' The crowd that was there and heard it said it had thundered; others said an angel had spoken to him. Jesus said, 'This voice was for your benefit, not mine. Now is the time for judgment on this world; now the prince of this world will be driven out. But I, when I am lifted up from the earth, will draw all men to myself.' He said this to show the kind of death he was going to die. The crowd spoke up, 'We have heard from the Law that the Christ will remain forever, so how can you say, 'The Son of Man must be lifted up'? Who is this 'Son of Man'?*

*Then Jesus told them, "You are going to have the light just a little while longer. Walk while you have the light, before darkness overtakes you. The man who walks in the dark does not know where he is going. Put your trust in the light while you have it, so that you may become sons of light.' When he had finished speaking, Jesus left and hid himself from them."*

Philip asked Jesus to see the Greeks. Without a doubt, as Jesus talked with them Philip observed the Oneness that existed between Jesus and His Father. Philip heard Jesus' voice change from tones of sorrow to tones of triumph. "*Now the prince of this world will be driven out. But I, when I am lifted up from the earth, will draw all men to myself.*"

And that brings us to the last scene. Philip said, "Could You just show us Your Father?" Looking back over these events of the recent past Jesus looked into Philip's face and asked, "Philip, have I been with you so long a time and still you do not know Me?" Behind Jesus question lay all of these events. "Philip, when you first saw me, did you not have the conviction that in Me was embodied the law and all righteousness? When you watched Me feed men did you not *understand that I can satisfy all the hungers of the human heart? When you saw me walk on water, didn't you see the authority I hold over nature? When you observed that strange time when you brought the Greeks to Me, didn't you understand that I am moving toward indescribable pain and anguish so that men can be set free?"*

But the truth was that Philip had not seen those things. He had observed them, but he had not seen them. He had eyes, but he did not see. He had ears, but he did not hear. He had not seen or heard because he had not understood. It was not until after Jesus had gone to the cross, after His resurrection, after the coming of the Holy Spirit at Pentecost, that Philip saw and heard it all. Then Philip understood, and it was then that Philip found that having seen Jesus he had seen the Father.

In looking upon One who in His own personality embodied all the facts of the law and of righteousness, He had seen the Father. In looking upon One who could touch the lunch of a lad and provide food for a multitude, and then to see Him deal with the spiritual needs of hungry hearts, he realized that he had seen the Father. In looking upon One who shrank from sorrow and yet pressed into it because He was at One with the purposes of His Father in His desire to rescue humanity, he had seen the Father. This was Jesus as He was revealed to mankind. This was God revealed to us as our Heavenly Father, and we see the value of the coming of Jesus in that amazing revelation of God.

What does that revelation mean to us? What does it mean to you? What would our lives be like if Jesus had never come to show us the Father? What ideas would mankind hold of God? What ideas would we hold of God? Would we have dismissed Him as dead, yet fear Him as well? In other religions, we see the gods that men have crafted. What would our god be like if Jesus had never come?

That leads us to our next question. Do we see Him today? He is with us, but do we see Him? Does He say to us, *"Have I been with you so long a time, and still you do not know me?"* He is here. He is at work in and through every circumstance of our lives. He is fulfilling His promise to make all things work together for good making us more like Christ. He is completing the good work He began long ago in our lives and in the lives of those we love. Why don't we see it? Why don't we recognize Him?

I thought about this a lot. I think it is a lack of spiritual awareness. We bring to every life experience our own interpretations and our own expectations. When our interpretations simply fail us, and when our expectations are not met we are disappointed and confused. Then we can't see God because we don't understand. Yet it is more than that. It is not that we can't understand. It is that we don't understand. Why would that be?

All too often we don't take time to look for what is hidden that lies behind what is revealed. Life is barreling on. We are forging ahead. It is tomorrow, and we have already forgotten the wonder, yes, the miracles, of yesterday! Then, we are blinded by reactive habits that for years have made up the fabric of our lives. These may go back generations. They are ways of reacting to the unexpected, and to disappointments and confusion and disaster. Our mothers and grandmothers and great grandmothers reacted the same way, and often the reactions are of anger and doubt and fear. If the truth be known, we don't know any other way to react. That is all we have ever seen. That has been our entire life experience. When times of crisis come, be they large or small, we have been programmed to react in certain ways. We find ourselves returning to those habits over and over again. It is not that we can't understand and see things differently and do things differently, but it may be that we just don't understand.

Finally, we are blinded by our lack of praise and thanksgiving in all things, for in all things we should be constantly awakening to new wonders of God's Love and grace and thanking Him. His revelations are here in the midst of our greatest heartaches, and our deepest needs and our most overwhelming fears, and we should offer our praise for the goodness of God. Such times offer us opportunities to experience God in ways that are ever new. Then we come to know Him better and to love Him more! Are there areas of your life today in which Jesus would kindly look into your eyes and say, *"Have I been with you so long and still you do not know me?"*

The response God calls us to never varies. We are to keep our eyes on Jesus, the author and finisher of our faith. We are to trust God in all things and honor Him as holy in the sight of all men, especially our family and friends. God is working miracles! We must look for them every day. We must expect them! We must recognize them! Often the miracle does not lie in a change of circumstances. Rather, it lies in us and in our perspective and response. The times of greatest testing offer us opportunities for the greatest triumphs.

Our Father sees us. He knows our needs. He hears our prayers. He answers us, always in love, in mercy, in grace and in faithfulness. His answer is determined by our response. It may be further discipline, but it is always given in Great Love!

Jesus came to destroy the works of the devil, to take away our sins and to show us The Father. Every day we are given the opportunity to offer Him our love and to surrender our hearts to Him. Those are the demands which His coming places upon us. May our paradigm change so that we see Him in all things, for He is in all! May we look into His face in reverence and awe. May we find our rest in Him, and may our hearts be fully satisfied as we see God, Our Father, in Jesus, the Christ.

## *Who Do You Say I Am?*

"Who do you say I am?" He asks.
Down through the eons of time
That question is put to every heart,
To your heart as well as to mine.
"The Son of the Living God," I cry;
"God's own Son, our Savior Divine!"
And He answers, "Then let me live My Life through you,
Give me your life, and I'll give you Mine."

## *Think on These Things*

Why do you think the claim Jesus made in our text marked Him for execution?

How would you define the Old Testament Hebrew conception of God as it was presented here, and how did it impact the morality of the nation?

How does the conception the world holds of Christianity affect today's wide spread attitude toward it?

In what way did the coming of Jesus reveal a completely new understanding of God?

How would you explain the concept of the Fatherhood of God?




What is it that sets Christianity apart from every other religion?




List the four times that we know of when Philip was seen with Jesus?

How was Philip involved in each of these occasions, and what do we know of his response to them?

Why do you think Philip did not see or hear or understand more truth concerning Jesus?

Can you share some of the ways you experience God as your Father?

Can you identify ways in which old patterns blind you to God's participating presence in your life?

Comment on your practice of praise and thanksgiving in all things. Is that a habit for you, or is it pretty foreign to your ways of thinking and responding?

Are you aware of a need to shift your paradigm and adopt a different perspective for how you are living your life?

I think you will enjoy reading and thinking about John 15:1-17.

# *Lesson 4*
## *Finding New Beginnings*

TEXT: *"The fear of the Lord is the beginning of wisdom, and knowledge of the Holy One is understanding."*

**Proverbs 9:10, NIV**

There are days and hours that speak to us of new beginnings. There are birthdays and school graduation days and wedding days. There are the days of moving to a new house or to a different state or country. There are days when new work is undertaken.

There are days that feel like endings that force us to new beginnings. There are hurt feelings and misunderstandings and divorces and illnesses and disability and death. All of these circumstances force us to start again from a different place. How full of change this life is, and change in all of its forms always involves new beginnings.

There are a number of expressions we use for new beginnings. We say that we turn over a new leaf or that we begin a new chapter. As we think about beginnings we often find ourselves wanting somehow to make the new chapter better than the last one. We may find ourselves looking back and seeing our mistakes. Sometimes they were willful mistakes, and sometimes they were made out of ignorance; but we earnestly desire to do better. We find ourselves genuinely seeking more strength, more faith, more hope, more order, more love, more truth.

But where should we begin? If we are serious, this is not a simple question. For one thing, new beginnings often give birth to new fears, and it is possible that the older we become the more afraid we become. Why would this be?

Perhaps it is because in the past we have set our heart to new beginnings. We hoped for better, and things got worse. We made resolutions, and we could not keep them. We may have been appalled to discover that when push came to shove we didn't even want to keep them! Still, we would like to think that it is not too late, and that we can begin again. But how?

An answer is found in our text. Proverbs 9:10 says, *"The fear of the Lord is the beginning of wisdom."* What does this mean to us, and how can we find here the key to a new chapter, a new page, a true new beginning?

We will begin our meditation by focusing our attention on two similar verses found in Proverbs. The first verse we will consider is found in Proverbs 1:7 and it reads, *"The fear of the Lord is the beginning of knowledge, but fools despise wisdom and instruction."* The second one is our text, Proverbs 9:10.

You might think that I would draw attention to the difference in the words *"knowledge"* and *"wisdom"*; but instead we are going to consider the word *"beginning"*. Each of these verses contain that word. In English, we appear to be dealing with one word, but in Hebrew we discover two different meanings here.

In the first declaration from Proverbs 1:7, *"beginning"* is a word that means first in order. It means to be at the beginning of the line, or first in a sequence of time. It means to be first in rank, or first in value, or first in importance. The thought being expressed in this declaration is that the fear of the Lord is the most important aspect of wisdom.

The meaning found in our text, Proverbs 9:10, is more exclusive. It refers specifically to the beginning as the starting point! The starting point to knowing wisdom is to have the fear of the Lord. The fear of the Lord is the abiding secret of the way of wisdom.

What is *"the fear of the Lord"*? This is an ancient statement. What does it have to do with us? What does it mean to us? How can it impact our lives?

The fear this verse speaks of is the recognition of God's Power and Might and Holiness. It is the admission in our hearts of the rightness of the claim He makes on us. It is a desire above all for His will in our lives. The fear of the Lord is submission and surrender and obedience to Him. It is not about professing truths about God. It is not about subscribing to creeds men have written about Him. It is possible to do these things without the fear of the Lord. This fear acknowledges God for who He is. It reverences Him by seeking His will and His ways in all things. The fear of the Lord puts us into right adjustment with Him as the eternal and infinite truth of the universe and of all life.

Now, what is the way of wisdom? It is the ability to understand what is right, true, and enduring. It is accurate judgment and sharp discernment in all things.

Let's return to the subject of beginnings, and in doing so we need to recognize that a beginning is never really a beginning. There is a past. There is something that preceded what we are calling a beginning.

We can find illustrations of this in any realm. For example, let's take a tree. What is the beginning of a tree? It is easy to see that its beginning relates to a past history.

I saw an example of this when I went out to get the mail and ran into my neighbor. She showed me three lime trees that were growing in her yard. One was bearing fruit, and she gave me one of the limes. This is the amazing part — she had grown these lime trees from seeds! She had planted lime seeds in her front yard, and the trees grew and are producing fruit!

However, the lime seeds were not the beginnings of those trees. The beginnings were the trees from which the seeds came, and we could follow that path back to discover that every single tree on this planet is related to mysteries that are infinite and far reaching. Every beginning points to an earlier beginning that points to a still earlier beginning. All of this relates back to that age-old question, "Which came first, the chicken or the egg?" As we begin to journey back we discover that "a" beginning is not really "the" beginning.

It is also true that morally there is no beginning either of sinning or of being righteous. We don't begin to sin when we sin. Behind the sinful act was the conception, the idea, the thought; and behind that, the temptations that assault the soul; and behind that the generational patterns we grew up with; and beyond that ... and beyond that ... and where is the beginning?

It is also true that there are no beginnings for doing right. The thought comes before the deed; and behind the thought lies the will; and behind the will, the examples we grew up with; and behind that ... Where is the beginning?

Form of being may have a beginning, but that which takes a new form existed before in another form. The new form is the result of the history that lies behind the old form. The new form evolves out of the past.

A great example from the realm of nature takes place each year in my back yard. Every spring I plant parsley hoping to attract the black swallowtail butterfly. It likes to lay its tiny, almost microscopic eggs on parsley.

If I see a black swallowtail flitting around my parsley, I know that within days, if I look closely, I will find the tiniest little caterpillars you can imagine. They are barely larger than a period at the end of a sentence. Then they start eating, and before long I begin to wonder if I will have enough parsley to feed them! However, before I know it, they have entered the pupa stage that culminates with the emergence of a gorgeous butterfly. The butterfly emerged in a new form, but it previously existed in another form. The new form evolved out of all that was before.

Nicodemus had a tremendous sense of his past the night he looked into Jesus' eyes and asked Him, *"How can someone be born when they are old?"* (John 3:4). It was a question that was not flippant, rude or irrelevant. It rose up out of the deepest recess of his soul. What of the years that had run their course? How does a person begin again?

The past must be taken into account, because a beginning is never the beginning. However, God tells us that out of our past, He creates new forms. As we allow Him and trust Him, He weaves a beautiful tapestry out of our lives. He holds the power to work all together for good!

We have the promise of Romans 8:28-29. *"And we know that in all things God works for the good of those who love him, who have been called according to his purpose. For those God foreknew he also predestined to be conformed to the likeness of his Son, that he might be the firstborn among many brothers."*

We are assured by Paul's words in Philippians 1:3-6. *"I thank my God every time I remember you. In all my prayers for all of you, I always pray with joy because of your partnership in the gospel from the first day until now, being confident of this, that he who began a good work in you will carry it on to completion until the day of Christ Jesus."*

Henri Nouwen wrote in his book *Here and Now: Living in the Spirit*[2] that every moment is a new beginning.

He writes, "A new beginning! We must learn to live each day, each hour, yes, each minute as a new beginning, as a unique opportunity to make everything new. Imagine that we could live each moment as a moment pregnant with new life. Imagine that we could live each day as a day full of promises. Imagine that we could walk through the new year always listening to a voice saying to us; 'I have a gift for you and can't wait for you to see it!' Imagine.

Is it possible that our imagination can lead us to the truth of our lives? Yes, it can! The problem is that we allow our past, which becomes longer and longer each year, to say to us: 'You know it all. You have seen it all. Be realistic. The future will be just another repeat of the past. Try to survive it as best you can.' There are many cunning foxes jumping on our shoulders and whispering in our ears the great lie; 'There is nothing new under the sun . . . don't let yourself be fooled.'

When we listen to these foxes, they eventually prove themselves right. Our new year, our new day, our new hour becomes flat, boring, dull, and without anything new.

So, what are we to do? First, we must send the foxes back to where they belong; in their foxholes. And then we must open our minds and our hearts to the voice that resounds through the valleys and hills of our life saying, *"Let me show you where I live among my people. My name is God with you. I will wipe away all the tears from your eyes; there will be no more death, and no more mourning or sadness. The world of the past has gone"* (Revelation 21:2-5).

We must choose to listen to that voice, and every choice will open us a little more to discover the new life hidden in the moment, waiting eagerly to be born."

I read Nouwen's essay every morning for a year, and it changed the way I was living my life! I became intensely aware of the new beginnings that reside in every hour; new beginnings that take the past into account, but out of which beautiful new patterns can emerge.

Then, we must recognize that a beginning is not a self-contained event. Whatever begins, begins in an environment that is affected by outside forces. Some of these forces will be destructive, and some will be constructive.

I saw this truth in action watching the caterpillars. I had been surprised to find three caterpillars on our parsley. Two had grown quite large. Then rain storms came through, and when they had passed there was only one small caterpillar left. Had driving rain washed the other two away? I don't know. But one thing is certain — the storms that rolled through acted on those caterpillars. After the storm, a bit of sunshine smiled on the remaining one, and I saw that it was busily munching away on the fresh green parsley.

The environment that the caterpillars grow in may nourish them to greater strength that can enable them to evolve to the perfection of their being, but at the same time there are forces within their environment that can destroy them. If they are able to survive what is destructive and respond and thrive under the influence of what is constructive, then they will reach the fulfillment of their destiny.

As we leave this realm of nature and consider our own lives, we can immediately see how true these principles are for us, too. We initiate our new beginnings in the midst of forces that are both constructive and destructive. They are here with us now! We cannot turn over a new leaf alone. We cannot begin independently. Our past is with us, and our new beginning is never self-contained. There will always be forces that descend upon us. Some would build us up and some would tear us down.

In the spiritual realm, new beginnings readjust our lives to these forces. The better part of wisdom will take them into account. Then we make our choices. We can close our lives to much that tears down, and we can open them to much that builds up. But that leads us back to the question of how to begin, and even to the question of whether or not we can begin. We ask again, is it true that a new beginning is never a new beginning? We have seen that this is a true statement, but it is just as true to say that a new beginning is a new beginning, for when we start new things, we begin. When life is expressed in a new way, forces are set in motion that the eye cannot see. Just consider the conception of a baby! When we make a new start, when we mount a new beginning, for better or for worse we set in motion forces that will move on from there.

This creates a supreme responsibility. When we turn our lives toward things that are morally low and disgraceful and destructive we set in motion forces that we do not have control over. We cannot see what their ultimate, future expression will be.

When James first started working in the construction business, one of his co-workers was seen as the golden boy of the company. He was smart, likeable and easy to work with. He had a lovely family. James considered himself fortunate to be able to work with him.

As superintendent, he had already been with the company for more than 20 years, but before long we began to hear rumblings that his wife had left him; then, that he was drinking too much. Then came the day that he didn't show up for work. James found him dead drunk in a cheap motel. That was the day our friend lost his job. He had not been able to admit to himself when he started enjoying a beer every day after work that he was, in fact, an alcoholic. No one was able convince him that what he had set in motion would eventually cost him everything.

It is just as true that when we choose on the side of good, we initiate a momentum for good that the future will fulfill. The things that follow will grow out of that beginning. The days to come will be shaped by what we started.

The long-term effects of the beginnings we choose and the forces they put into motion can hardly be calculated. They will play out in every area of our lives. For example, medical researchers have long told us that psychological factors can play a part in causing disease — all the way from colds to cancer. Researchers now have some information about the way thoughts and moods set in motion a ballet of hormones, neurotransmitters and nerve cell activity that has a subtle, but telling effect on physical health.

How can we give right direction, shape, form and expression to our future? How can we know the transformation we are promised; from glory to glory? In 2 Corinthians 3:18 we read, *"And we, who with unveiled faces all reflect the Lord's glory, are being transformed into his likeness with ever-increasing glory, which comes from the Lord, who is the Spirit."* How can this be our life experience? We must find a way to establish a right relationship: first, with the past; second, with the present forces of our environment; and finally, with the unknown and unforeseeable future.

Is there a principle of action we need to turn to? It must be a fundamental truth or law on which others are based. It must reach beyond the intellectual confirmation of religious beliefs. It must surpass theory. It must be more than a philosophy. It must be rooted in reality and spirituality. It must be a principle that, if observed, will allow us to live out of a place of moral strength that rightly distinguishes between right and wrong; between truth and falsehood. It must hold out to us well founded hope for a righteous and Godly future.

This brings us full circle, back to our text, Proverbs 9:10. *"The fear of Jehovah is the beginning of wisdom."* Herein lies our principle.

Now, who is Jehovah? Who is the Lord? The only answer we have is that of Biblical revelation. The answer is threefold. First, He is the Creator and He knows perfectly all that He has created. Second, He is the Preserver — He preserves and cares for all He has created. Finally, He is the Redeemer — He redeems because He loves all that He has created and preserved. As we put our lives into right relationship with The Creator, The Preserver and The Redeemer — we will start a true new beginning.

As the Creator, He knows us perfectly. We see the truth of this in Psalm 139:1-6:

*"You have searched me Lord,*
*and you know me.*
*You know when I sit and when I rise;*
*you perceive my thoughts from afar.*
*You discern my going out and my lying down;*
*you are familiar with all my ways.*
*Before a word is on my tongue*
*you know it completely.*
*You hem me in behind and before;*
*you lay your hand upon me.*
*Such knowledge is too wonderful for me,*
*too lofty for me to attain."*

The Lord understands my thoughts from afar. Thought is an amazing thing, mysterious and strange. It often puzzles me. Through my thoughts, temptation assaults me. Through my thoughts, high aspirations come to me. Often, I do not understand my own thoughts, but the Lord knows and understands them.

It is interesting to know that we are the realized thoughts of God. Imagine that! He thought us. He planned us. He created us. He breathed into us the breath of life. He sees us. He watches over us. He understands everything about our beings. He knows all about us physically. We are *"fearfully and wonderfully made"* (Psalm 139:14). He understands our mental capacities. He knows how we learn, and how that fits us uniquely for the life He planned for us to live. He understands the deep spiritual parts of us, and the mysterious and wonderful ways we are connected to Him. We don't fully know ourselves, but the Lord knows us perfectly.

Not only is He The Creator. He is also The Preserver. He didn't create us and then leave us to ourselves. He cares for us. *"Cast all your anxiety on him because he cares for you"* (1 Peter 5:7).

It is right here that we encounter difficulties. Have you ever felt that God did not care? Haven't we all encountered situations in which we questioned God's care? We must grant that there are times when it is hard to believe that God always cares.

In considering that, we must realize that there is a plane of human suffering from which God is excluded because of human rebellion. God has granted every human being free will, and He will not violate it. It would not be free will if He did. However, that leaves us with a plane of suffering that is not relieved by the power of God because men have excluded Him. Lack of provision from God is not to blame, but the way mankind has handled His provision. When men turn their backs on God and ignore His laws and reject His ways, suffering follows; and often the innocent are caught up in the suffering. Still, He stands over the sands of time as the Preserver of all who call on Him. *"Have I not commanded you? Be strong and courageous. Do not be terrified; do not be discouraged, for the Lord your God will be with you wherever you go"* (Joshua 1:9).

Finally, He is The Redeemer. We are all too familiar with the problem of evil. It exists, and has touched every life. Mankind has lost the vision of God, the consciousness of God and a relationship with God. When this happens evil surges through societies, destroying lives. Left to our own devises we are all rebels. In resisting and opposing God, consciousness of Him is lost. It is not that God has abandoned us, but that we have abandoned Him. He is with us always, associating Himself with sinning souls so that they may be healed and restored to fellowship with Him. The cost to Him cannot be measured.

One way or another, our lives are being lived out in adjustment to what we believe. If God is The Creator, common sense determines that we will try to discover what it is that He created us for. If He is The Preserver, the primary business of life is to recognize and honor and cooperate with His faithfulness. If He is The Redeemer, then the business to which He has called us is to yield to His redemption.

One of the enduring blessings of the Christian life is that it offers us the only way in this life to find bright and true new beginnings. He offers us a new life. Spirits that were born dead in that they were separated from God can be born again into Oneness with Him. Then God takes the old forms and makes of them something beautiful and new.

In John 1:12 we read:

*"Yet to all who received him, to those who believed in his name, he gave the right to become children of God — children born not of natural descent nor of human decision or a husband's will, but born of God."*

In Ephesians 1:15-19, Paul offers this beautiful prayer:

*"For this reason, ever since I heard about your faith in the Lord Jesus and your love for all God's people, I have not stopped giving thanks for you, remembering you in my prayers. I keep asking that the God of our Lord Jesus Christ, the glorious Father, may give you the Spirit of wisdom and revelation, so that you may know him better. I pray also that the eyes of your heart may be enlightened in order that you may know the hope to which he has called you, the riches of his glorious inheritance in his holy people, and his incomparably great power for us who believe.*

Proverbs 9:10 states, *"The fear of the Lord is the beginning of wisdom, and knowledge of the Holy One is understanding."* Lives of wisdom and beauty will unfold and develop out of the fear, the awareness and the reverence that brings us to acknowledge God in all things. Our lives are lived in adjustment to what we believe. May they reflect the beauty of the Lord our God!

## Live to Your Honor

To live to the honor of Your glory
To live to Your honor, I pray.
To live to the honor of Your glory!
That's my prayer, and the promise of today.

# *Think on These Things*

Explain how new beginnings often give birth to new fears.




Discuss the different meanings of the word "beginning", first as it is used in Proverbs 1:7 and secondly as it is used in Proverbs 9:10.




Explain the meaning of the word translated "beginning" as we discussed in this lesson.




Why is a beginning never truly a beginning?

Can you give an example of God creating new forms out of our past?




What is it that new beginnings do for us?




Give an example of how form and expression have new beginnings.




What is meant by *"the fear of the Lord"*?

Who is Jehovah?

Discuss the ideas of God as the Creator, the Preserver and the Redeemer.

How is it true that our lives are lived out in adjustment to what we believe?

I think you will enjoy reading and thinking about Proverbs Chapter 8.

# *Lesson 5*
## Have You Decided to Follow Jesus?

TEXT: *"I will follow you, Lord; but ..."*

**Luke 9:61, NIV**

We will begin here with the Scripture reading from which our lesson is taken, Luke 9:46-62:

> *An argument started among the disciples as to which of them would be the greatest. Jesus, knowing their thoughts, took a little child and had him stand beside him. Then he said to them, "Whoever welcomes this little child in my name welcomes me; and whoever welcomes me welcomes the one who sent me. For it is the one who is least among you all— he is the greatest."*
>
> *"Master," said John, "we saw someone driving out demons in your name and we tried to stop him, because he is not one of us."*
>
> *"Do not stop him" Jesus said, "for whoever is not against you is for you."*
>
> *As the time approached for him to be taken up to heaven, Jesus resolutely set out for Jerusalem. And he sent messengers on ahead, who went into a Samaritan village to get things ready for him; but the people there did not welcome him, because he was heading for Jerusalem.*
>
> *When the disciples James and John saw this, they asked, "Lord, do you want us to call fire down from heaven to destroy them?"*

*But Jesus turned and rebuked them, and they went to another village.*

*As they were walking along the road, a man said to him, "I will follow you wherever you go."*

*Jesus replied, "Foxes have dens and birds of the air have nests, but the Son of Man has no place to lay his head."*

*He said to another man, "Follow me."*

*But the man replied, "Lord, first let me go and bury my father."*

*Jesus said to him, "Let the dead bury their own dead, but you go and proclaim the kingdom of God."*

*Still another said, "I will follow you, Lord; but first let me go back and say good-bye to my family."*

*Jesus replied, "No one who puts a hand to the plow and looks back is fit for service in the kingdom of God."*

When the events took place that are recorded for us here in the Book of Luke, Jesus had set his face toward Jerusalem. These days were days that tested all human relationships, and they were days of crisis.

As a boy growing up in Nazareth Jesus was beloved by those who knew Him. *Luke* tells us that *"the child grew and became strong; he was filled with wisdom, and the grace of God was on him"* (Luke 2:40). In the early days of His ministry He was sought out. Attention centered on Him. All kinds of people came out to see Him and hear Him. However, as He began to teach truth, righteousness, and purity people began to fall away. Now, as He moved into these last few weeks leading up to His crucifixion, all human relationships that He sustained moved through a time of trial and of crisis.

Jesus' own disciples were jockeying for position in His coming kingdom, and arguing over which of them was the greatest. John was upset because someone outside the group of disciples had been teaching in the name of Jesus. John could not say that the man was not following Christ, only that he was not following along with the disciples. The Samaritans refused Jesus entrance into one of their villages. We could extend this list, but such were the things that Jesus was contending with.

All the while His face was set toward Jerusalem. Jerusalem! The city that He knew so well. The city that He loved. He knew that now it was waiting for Him, waiting to arrest Him, waiting to kill Him. We know that it was somewhere on this journey toward Jerusalem that the events we are considering took place.

We know that one man, out of the fullness of his heart it would seem, said to Jesus, *"I will follow you wherever You go."* We know that further along the way, Jesus called to another man saying, *"Follow me."* We know that a third man, seemingly less impulsive than the first said, *"I will follow you, Lord; but first let me bid farewell to those who are in my house."* It is here that we find our text for this lesson.

To the first of these men the Lord said in effect, "You say to me that you will follow me wherever I go, but do you know what my life is like?" In Luke 9:58 Jesus says, *"The foxes have dens, and the birds have nests; but the Son of man does not have a place to lay His head."*

The second man, the one that Jesus called to follow Him, declined on the basis of his duty as a son. It is understood that when he said to Jesus that he needed to go and bury his father, his father was still very much alive. He wasn't asking for time to go attend a funeral. He was asking for time to return home until his father died. He was putting his obligations as a son ahead of his calling from Jesus.

To the third man who wanted to go say goodbye to those at home Jesus responded with the priority of His claim by saying, *"No one who puts his hand to the plow, and looks back is fit for service in the kingdom of God"* (Luke 9:62).

These incidents constitute the background against which our lesson is constructed. Did any or all of these men ultimately follow Christ? We do not know. What we do know is what this passage reveals. First, there is the call of Christ and the supremacy of that call. Second, we see that difficulties present themselves to the minds of many who would follow Jesus, and the difficulties are very real and definite. Third, the passage teaches us the urgency of an immediate decision. We see that it is out of place to count the cost. This is the opposite of the wisdom of this world, which is to always count the cost before we act. Jesus' call is to follow Him, and to follow immediately whatever the cost may be. That is obedience in action!

Before we consider these points, we are going to spend a few minutes on this word *"follow"*. Jesus' favorite way of calling men to Himself was simply to use two words; *"Follow Me."* This call was repeated over and over again. He used it to call out His initial invitation to join Him in His work. He used it to call His own apostles to higher service. He often made use of these simple words: *"Follow Me."* Confronting someone who was busy with their daily occupation, He would look into their eyes and say, *"Follow Me."* It was an invitation to put trust in Him, to have confidence in Him, to obey Him. To this day it is His claim of supreme authority, and He calls us to submit to it.

But there is more here than a call to submission in response to His claim of supremacy. These two little words infer guidance and victory. They infer that Jesus knows the way, and that He has the ability to direct to the highest and best fulfillment of life. *"Follow Me"* is still Christ's Word to every one of us! It is the one thing He says to every person with no regard for race or creed. It is a universal call. It is His open invitation. *"Come and follow Me."*

This call assumes His ability to lead, to guide and to deliver. It is a call that declares His authority; and He insists that those who answer His call must believe in Him, and must demonstrate their belief by obedience. The words are brief, and so simple that even a child can understand them. Once they are spoken there is nothing more to be said. Obedience to those words are the first step in the life of a Christian, and they should define the entire experience of the Christian life. Finally, when the time comes for us to move into that other dimension of life — when we come to the hour of our death — even then we will simply be following Him.

However, it is not always that simple. There are difficulties that lie in the way. There are people who accept the claims of Jesus and hear His call, yet refuse to respond. They don't want to follow Him. They want to go their own way. They want to live their own way. They have their own plans and goals and purposes. We live in a society that would try to teach us the fine art of being in control. Voluntarily giving of control over to an invisible God feels like insanity, and these people have no intention of doing it.

Actually, believing that we have control over our lives is nothing but a grand illusion. I recall a conversation I had one day with my brother. He was an oncologist in Atlanta, Georgia, and he was talking to me about some of his patients. I have never forgotten one thing he said. "The ones who do the best in treatment are the ones who always understood that they never did have control of their lives. The ones who imagined that they were in control have a hard go of it."

Then, there is another group of people. They are the ones who reject His claims entirely and therefore have no interest in His call. This message is not directed to either of these groups. It is directed to yet another group; to people who are attracted to Jesus, and who admire Him. They are aware of their own needs and of His claims to be able to meet those needs. They want to follow Him. They intend to follow Him. They may have said many times, "I will follow You, Lord. I will follow You!" However, somehow the following never begins, and somewhere in the back of their minds they hold this thought, "I will follow You, Lord, but ..."

Perhaps they are genuinely afraid to follow Him. They have studied to attain a degree in their field of choice, but they hear Him calling them to service in other areas. They have been highly successful, and answering His call would require them to do something that would impact their material well-being. Added to that is the question of how the way will be made clear. They wonder how they can be sure of their calling. They understand today. The call is to obedience and surrender, but what of tomorrow? What will tomorrow hold?

How can that difficulty be answered? We could answer by citing Scriptures from the Old and the New Testament. We could be reminded that our works are foreordained by God. We could remember the children of Israel, and the way that God led them by a cloud during the day, and by a pillar of fire by night. God was always out ahead of them, and at night they pitched their tents in a place of His choosing. That is the ancient picture. We could bear witness to God's leading in our own lives. No one has ever been put to shame who has placed their trust in God. He leads us ever onward. The mists are dispelled before us, and we will never lose our way. This is the universal testimony of those who truly place their trust in Him.

Dr. Morgan once heard a young woman speak who told of the following experience. She was traveling in the Far East, and at a certain point in the trip a guide came to assume responsibility for the travelers and to lead them on their journey. The guide said to them, "Will you please give all that you have to me? I will take charge of everything." So, people began to hand over to him all of their suitcases and all of their luggage, but the women were hanging on to their purses.

The guide said again, "You must turn everything over to me." The women protested that they might need the things in their purses, but the guide replied that the purses would be much safer with him, and that they would be much safer without them.

Before long the travelers found themselves standing on the platform at the railway station while the guide attended to the baggage. A train rolled in, and the entire party boarded it. No sooner were they seated, than their guide returned. "Would you all please be good enough to follow me?" he asked. And then he promptly led them off the train. "What is wrong?" they asked. "Why did you get us off that train?" He replied, "That is the wrong train. From now on will you all be kind enough to follow after me and not go before me?"

The next several days were long and tiring, and everyone was anxiously awaiting arrival at their destination. Then some stranger, who had come through the town they were going to, told them that there were no accommodations there. The hotels were all full. There would be no place for them there. They all wondered, because their guide had said nothing about it. However, when they arrived everything was in readiness and accommodations had been prepared for them. It was then that the guide said quietly, "You can trust me to see that preparations are made ahead for you. You can trust me, if you will simply follow me."

This simple story illustrates the words of Jesus. He goes before us. He makes a way, even where there is no way.

Always, He says, "Follow Me." As our Guide, He says to us, "Entrust everything to me. Then don't go out ahead of Me. Follow behind Me."

"I will follow You, Lord, but ..." Surely it isn't necessary to give everything over to You. There are so many things that I really need. Surely it is enough to give myself to You, but You know that there are things I need to keep under my own control. There is my time and the way I use it. There is my money and the way I spend it. There are my friendships. There are my loves. I have my hopes and my dreams and my plans. I have given myself to You. Now, may I not keep these other things? Must You have authority over everything I possess? There are some things that I hold dear that I would have to give up. After all, there are many things that seem clear and plain to me. I really believe that my ideas are sound, and that my way is best, and that I am justified in moving forward.

This kind of self-centered thinking can lead one astray. True evil exists in the lives of some people. It may lie within friendships, habits or practices. All of these things have to go. Jesus said we must renounce all in order to be His disciples. His Word to us is that we will be far safer when He has charge of everything, and that our things will be infinitely safer with Him.

It is hard for some people to imagine bringing every decision to Christ. There are many who would say that they don't know how to surrender to God, and frankly, they don't believe they can do it. That is the story, perhaps for millions of people.

If we choose to surrender to God, exactly what are we asked to let go of? Perhaps the first thing is the right to steer our own lives. When we surrender, we put our lives into His hands. We allow Him to do the steering for us. That can be terrifying and at the same time, exhilarating. This is depicted in the following poem:

When I met Christ
it seemed as though life were rather like a bike ride,
but it was a tandem bike,
and I noticed that Christ
was in the back helping me pedal.

I don't know just when it was
that He suggested we change places,
but life has not been the same since.

When I had control,
I knew the way I wanted to go.
It was rather boring, and predicable . . .
But it was the shortest distance between two points.

But when He took the lead,
He knew delightful long cuts,
up mountains, and through rocky places
at breakneck speeds,
and it was all I could do to hang on!
Even though it looked like madness,
He said, "Pedal. Just pedal!"

I worried and was anxious and asked,
Where are you taking me?"
He laughed and said, "Trust me!"
and I started to learn trust.
I forgot my boring life and entered into the adventure.
When I'd say, "I'm scared,"
He'd lean back and touch my hand.

He took me to people with gifts that I needed,
Gifts of healing, and acceptance and joy.
Then He said, "Now give the gifts away;
Share the gifts with others.

They're extra baggage and too much weight."

So I did, to the people we met,
and I found that in giving I received
pressed down, and running over,
and our burden was light.

I did not trust Him, at first,
in control of my life.
I thought He'd wreck it;
but I found that He knows bike secrets.

He knows how to make the bends,
And how to take sharp corners.
He knows how to jump to clear high rocks,
He even knows how to fly to shorten scary passages.

And I am learning to shut up and pedal
In the strangest places;
and I've learned to enjoy the views
and the cool breeze on my face
and my delightful and constant companion,
Jesus Christ.

And when I'm sure that I cannot possibly
do any more, He flashes me a big smile and says,
"Trust me, and just pedal."
— *Author Unknown*

Wherever you find yourself on your Christian journey, you can count on this. Sooner or later you will come to a point where you will have to choose whether or not to let go of the handlebars and let Jesus navigate for you. That is the point where belief in Jesus becomes surrender to

Him. That is the precise point at which you will begin to see your prayers answered and your life changed.

Romans 12:1-2 calls us to surrender:

> *Therefore, I urge you, brothers and sisters, in view of God's mercy, to offer your bodies as living sacrifices, holy and pleasing to God — this is your true and proper worship. Do not conform to the pattern of this world, but be transformed by the renewing of your mind. Then you will be able to test and approve what God's will is — his good, pleasing and perfect will."*

The sad truth is that many religious leaders lead people to believe that surrender is not necessary. It is easier to issue a call to commitment than it is to make a call to surrender. Commitment can be defined as what we do for God. We stand at the center of commitment. Surrender is what we allow God to do through us. God stands at the center of surrender.

So, what must we surrender? We must surrender everything! As we walk the pathway of surrender and obedience we will discover for ourselves what we must let go of! The following list is only a partial one, but perhaps it will help you get started.

First, as I have already said, we must surrender the handlebars — our will. Next, we must surrender our idols — our other gods. What are our gods? They are any activities, ideas and people that take us away from God's best. Because they take our time and attention and money they keep us from becoming all that God would have us be.

I witnessed an example of this in a church I once attended — a church that held a Tuesday morning Bible study. A friend of mine taught it, and it was excellent. There was a woman who did not choose to attend, and she was very vocal as to why she did not come. That was her bridge day! Anytime someone talked about the blessing of the Bible study she would say, "Well, I'm sorry I missed that, but I simply can't miss my bridge day." There was a choice to be made, and she had made her choice. She would invest her time in the bridge club.

Philippians 2:12-13 reminds us that it is God who is working in us, helping us be able to do what is pleasing to Him.

> *"Therefore my dear friends, as you have always obeyed — not only in my presence, but now much more in my absence — continue to work out your salvation with fear and trembling, for it is God who works in you to will and to act according to his good purpose."*

God is at work in us, helping us to want what He wants! Our idols may be things that we want, and that we come to believe we need. Our things can exert tyranny over our lives. I had wonderful examples of generosity in that I grew up with people who held their possessions with open hands. If someone walked into my grandmother's house and admired something of hers, she would often say, "Honey, you just take that. It makes me happy to think of your enjoying it."

Once I received a phone call from one of my cousins. She asked if I had our grandmother's Little Red Riding Hood cookie jar. Then she asked me if it had some little flowers on it and several other questions that helped her make the determination that it was a very valuable collector's item. She said that she had been looking in antique stores for years to find a cookie jar just like Mama's, but she had never been able to find one.

I said, "Well, you come over here and get this one. I have enjoyed it for years, and it will make me happy for you to have it now." She later told me that a friend said to her,

"I can't believe Marjorie gave you that cookie jar." My cousin replied, "Well, she had a mother and a grandmother who would have given you anything in their houses!"

I tell this story to remind all of us that there are countless ways that we can bless others. One way is to demonstrate that our lives are not bound by the tyranny of things. A.W. Tozer wrote the following prayer of surrender:

> "Father, I want to know You, but my coward heart fears to give up its toys. I cannot part with them without inward bleeding, and I do not try to hide from You the terror of the parting. I come trembling, but I do come. Please root from my heart all those things which have become a part of my living self, so that You may enter and dwell there without a rival."

Our idols are things that for a time will fill our inner cravings. They are things that tranquilize our restlessness, and for a short time will seem to fill our empty spirits. These idols may be material things or relationships or activities or habits. They may not be the big, dramatic things that pass through our lives, but the mindless busyness and restless preoccupations that rob us of joy. There is a way of living that focuses on surface trivialities rather than on depths of spiritual surrender. It is a way of living that uses noise, food, television, the Internet, cell phones or text messages to anesthetize both boredom and pain, and to deceive us into feeling connected and in control. Tilden Edwards calls this the *"under-life"*. It has also been called the *"half-life"*. It is the living of an impoverished life that falls far short of all that is possible.

Surrender means that we cannot choose what we do or what we don't do. Surrender means that we cannot choose where to live, or who our friends will be, or how our time is spent.  It means that we consult God about everything.  We ask Him to choose His best for us, and we acknowledge that we don't know what that will look like. It may be all sunshine, or it may be a storm! It means that we are just as excited about the stormy days as we are about the peaceful ones.  It means we are just as excited about the doors He closes as we are about the doors He opens. This is how He makes His way clear, and these are the ways that we follow Him!

Twenty-five years ago, James and I sold a ranch we had in central Texas.  Owning it had been a dream come true! We ran cows on it. We raised and baled our own hay. We spent half of our time out there, and we loved it! Then, on my birthday, June 27, as we rounded our corner we saw that turkey houses were being built right across from our place.  Plantation Foods, the largest producer of turkey products in the state of Texas, was buying up land in our area. Needless to say, the air quality left much to be desired once the turkeys arrived!  Eventually, we sold our dream place to Plantation Foods.

We left there with every intention of returning to a life in the country.  Thus, began a search that lasted for years! We prayed that God would open the doors for us or close them according to His will.  The doors kept closing, and closing and closing! We put contracts on four different places and at the last minute and in the strangest ways each one fell through. Finally, it dawned on us that God's will for us was to stay right where we are!

Looking back with the hindsight that time provides we can see the many blessings of staying here in Fort Worth. We live on almost 2 acres with a year-round creek running through it.  Mother was with us for almost two years in a house that was well suited to having her.  It has offered unique opportunities for ministry.  We asked God to choose the place for us to live, and so far, this house that we have lived in for more than 40 years has been His choice for us.

There is also the matter of allowing God to choose our friends. When our children were little, I accepted a part-time job teaching kindergarten. For several years my life was so caught up in it that I had little time to connect with old friends. Then the day came when I left my job and once again became a full-time mom.

I decided to ask God to choose my friends for me. I prayed and promised Him that anyone who reached out to me, I would respond to. However, I would not make the first move. I would trust him to orchestrate the friendships He had in mind that could be to His honor and glory. That was one of the most interesting summers ever! Completely new people came into my life, and the relationships were fascinating! They covered the socioeconomic span from one extreme to the other. I found it so rewarding that to this day I have continued to open my life to the relationships God brings my way. That is where my efforts and focus lie.

Amazing surprises have come my way, and I have been spared much disappointment and heartache. It is not unusual for people who are involved in ministry to feel slighted and left out, even within their own churches. Special groups or cliques, if you will, form. Those who lead in ministry often find that they are not included, and it leads to loneliness and discouragement. Asking God to choose my friends has taken away all of that sadness. I speak from experience.

Some years ago, a group was formed made up of women I considered to be good friends. I respected and admired them, and I heard that they were meeting on a regular basis. However, I was not invited to join their group. There was a time when I would have been terribly disappointed. However, I can honestly say that there was none of that. What I felt was a sense of interest and excitement to see how God would bless their group, and curiosity to see who God would put me into relationships with.

When we are following Him even our time is not our own. We have only one life to live, and a limited number of days are allotted to us. We all know people who are being used by God in every arena imaginable. There are countless ways in which God can use the hours of each day to bring honor and glory to His name. We need to be sensitive to His leading.

What else must we surrender? We must surrender our losses. Life brings with it inevitable losses. Some are very large, and some are small. But this we know. Losses are never easy. Hopes may die. Dreams may remain unfulfilled. Death or divorce can enter our lives in dramatic ways. As we grow older, we look in the mirror every morning only to be reminded that we have lost our youth. Times, they are a changing, and we are changing too!

There is great peace to be found in surrendering our losses to Jesus. We can entrust them all to Him. As we allow Him to take them, we will experience comfort and healing.

It is also true that our past, our present and our future must be surrendered to God. In Matthew 6:34, Jesus encourages His followers to embrace each day, each hour, and each minute: *"Therefore, do not worry about tomorrow, for tomorrow will worry about itself. Each day has enough trouble of its own."* As creatures of time we have no choice but to live moment by moment, but we are constantly looking back at what was and forward to what we either hope or dread is yet to come.

There is amazing freedom to be experienced when we begin living in the present moment. The scholar and philosopher, Rabbi Abraham Joshua Heschel (1907-1972), wrote, "Who is worthy to be present at the constant unfolding of time? Amidst the meditation of mountains, the humility of flowers — clouds that die constantly for the sake of his glory . . . only one response can maintain us: gratefulness for witnessing the wonder." It is a demonstration of great wisdom to surrender to God in the present moment and to witness with wonder the ways in which each day unfolds.

Now we move on to the issue of surrendering our control over others. This is an issue all of us face. It is a tricky issue, for there are times when we are expected to be in control. I remember my mother saying in Sunday school that she had a brand-new granddaughter. She was watching how hard James and I were working to assume complete responsibility for that baby. She pointed out that we were going to have to provide her every need. We were going to teach her to eat, drink, walk and talk. She went on to say that one day we would have to lay down our responsibility for her, and that would be much harder than picking it up was.

We can all vouch for that, can't we? The day does come when we must put it all into God's hands. We must quit offering prayers that are little more than worrying in God's presence, and begin thanking Him for continuing to keep every promise. We surrender it all to Him!

I can no longer imagine wanting to be in control of my own life. I acknowledge that I couldn't be even if I wanted to; but if I could, it would scare me to death to step into that position. My trust lies with the One who said, *"If your son asks for bread, will you give him a stone? Or if he asks for fish will you give him a snake? If you, then, though you are evil, know how to give good gifts to your children, how much more so does your father who is in heaven?"* (Matthew 7:9-11).

Where are you today as far as surrender to God is concerned? Have you given all to Him? There is a foolproof way to know the answer to that question. Look into the depths of your being and see what you find there. If there is peace and hope and joy and quiet confidence then you have surrendered everything to Him. If there is fear or confusion or disappointment or disillusionment you still hold on to the central position in your life — you still want what you want!

*"Follow Me."* The invitation is personal. The call is genuine. The time is short. The matter is urgent.

In closing, I want to tell you of an experience that Henri Nouwen wrote about. He took his 88-year-old father to the circus. Nouwen was thrilled by the performance of a family of trapeze artists. At the intermission, Nouwen went over to talk with them. Out of that simple beginning, it was decided that Nouwen would spend his upcoming vacation traveling with them.

One evening Nouwen sat talking with the head of the family. This man said, "Henri, I can do triple somersaults, and I get all of the applause. However, I am not the hero of our act. The hero is our catcher. One of the greatest mistakes I can make is to reach for him. If I try to grab for him we could easily break one another's wrists. I must just do my triple and then close my eyes and go down, holding my arms out and trusting that I will be caught by the catcher."

Nouwen later wrote that we all have to do many "triples" every day, but we are not the heroes. God is the hero. He is our catcher. We surrender to Him when we reach out our arms and trust Him to catch us. We can pray as Jesus did on the cross: "Father, into your hands I commit my spirit" (Luke 23:46). This is the joy and freedom of the surrendered Christian Life. This is the wonder of following Jesus!

He places a claim on human life that is supreme. He calls us to follow Him with our whole hearts. Following Him will bring us to the highest purpose for our lives. This is one of the greatest blessings of the Christian life for it will lead to a glorious realization of God's best, and He waits for our answer.

Are you following Him every hour of every day? If not, why not? I will follow You, Jesus, BUT … What is the "but" for you? Against what comes after that "but" you must fling all the force of your will and all of your resolve. It is our will and our choice whether or not to follow. In His strength may we gladly say, "I will follow You, Lord. Wherever You lead me, I will follow."

Then what? Then His own dear name will be glorified. My life shall be fully and completely realized, and I will live out my days at His disposal for helpfulness and love to others as I share with them the Kingdom of God.

## *I Will Follow You, Lord*

I will follow You, Lord,
I'll follow You today.
I will follow You, Lord,
Every step of the way.
When the sun is shining
And happiness marks my way,
I will follow You, Lord,
I'll follow You all the way.

I'll follow You in the morning,
I'll follow you at noon.
I'll follow You in the evening,
And through the night time gloom.
And when the storm clouds gather,
And darkness hides my way;
Still I'll follow You, Lord,
Every step of the way.

I will follow You, Lord,
I'll follow You always.
I will follow you Lord,
No matter what others say.
And when life's shadows lengthen
And life here is slipping away,
Then I will follow You, Lord,
'Till dawns the eternal day.

## *Think on These Things*

How is it that two little words, "Follow Me," define our calling as Christians?

Explain why it is so important to follow.

What difficulties present themselves to you when you contemplate following Jesus? What would be the most difficult thing for you to give up?

Why is it inappropriate to count the cost?

When the words "Follow Me" are spoken by Jesus, what promise do they hold?

Can you explain how these two words should define the entire experience of the Christian life?

Define the difference in commitment and surrender.

List as many things as possible that hold people back from surrendering to God.

Why is surrender necessary?

Explain how you can know whether or not you have surrendered all to Jesus.

Where will He lead you?

I think you will enjoy reading and thinking about Philippians 3:13-14, Matthew 6:19-34 and 2 Timothy 4:7-8.

## Lesson 6
### *What Is Our Part in The Christian Life?*
### *What Is God's Part?*

TEXT: *"So I went down to the potter's house, and I saw him working at the wheel."*

**Jeremiah 18:3, NIV**

There are two sides to a life and walk of faith. There is our part and there is God's part. Many Christians think and dwell exclusively on one side or the other, and that results in a distorted view of what the Christian life should be. That perspective produces disappointment, disillusionment and confusion. Both sides must be held constantly in mind, for undue emphasis on either part causes neglect of the other.

In her book *The Christian's Secret of a Happy Life*, Hannah Whitall Smith writes of attending a Bible conference in which one teacher spoke only of God's part in the Christian life, and another taught only of man's part. Many of their audience understood they were teaching two sides of the same great truth, but for others it was perplexing. One woman commented that she was confused. "These men seem to be flatly contradicting one another," she said. This confusion exists in the minds of many who seek spiritual truth.

What is our part, and what is God's part? I remember a time when that was a perplexing question for me, and it is always a critical question for us to address. To put it in its simplest terms, our part is to trust and God's part is to work; but what in the world does that mean as we live out our lives day by day?

When we begin living the life of a born-again Christian, there is a lot of work to be accomplished in our lives. God has promised to deliver us from the power of sin. He has promised change from the inside out. Our minds are to be renewed. Evil habits are to be overcome. Bad temper is to be controlled. A transformation, a complete metamorphosis is to take place. The truth of this is presented in Ephesians 2: 1-10:

*"As for you, you were dead in your transgressions and sins, in which you used to live when you followed the ways of this world and of the ruler of the kingdom of the air, the spirit who is now at work in those who are disobedient. All of us also lived among them at one time, gratifying the cravings of our flesh and following its desires and thoughts. Like the rest, we were by nature deserving of wrath. But because of his great love for us, God, who is rich in mercy, made us alive with Christ even when we were dead in transgressions — it is by grace you have been saved. And God raised us up with Christ and seated us with him in the heavenly realms in Christ Jesus, in order that in the coming ages he might show the incomparable riches of his grace, expressed in his kindness to us in Christ Jesus. For it is by grace you have been saved, through faith — and this not from yourselves, it is the gift of God — not by works, so that no one can boast. For we are God's handiwork, created in Christ Jesus to do good works which God prepared in advance for us to do."*

Now, someone must do this work! Either we must do it for ourselves or someone must do it for us. Many try to do this for themselves, and they fail miserably. For me there was a defining moment of failure. It came one night not long after our son, Mark, was born. After five long years of longing and praying for a baby we were blessed with two in one year. Lynn was born on December 1 of 1960, and Mark was born on December 17 of 1961. I faced motherhood with all the confidence in the world. Looking back, I realize it was the bliss of total ignorance!

The truth was that I had never been around a baby in all my life, but I had been teaching school for five years. I had faithfully attended parenting classes during my pregnancy. Now I considered myself good to go! After all, how hard could mothering be?

Reality soon came crashing in on me! Overwhelmed and exhausted there came a night when I sat on the back step sobbing my heart out. I had received what I wanted so desperately, but I didn't have the skills and the wisdom to handle it. I was trying so hard, but I could not be the mother, the wife or the person I wanted to be. That night I knew that it was simply not in me. It was not in me to be that person. It was a terrible feeling, and I have never forgotten it!

It was not long before I was reminded that Scripture tells us that apart from God, we can do nothing that is pleasing to Him. In John 5:19 we read: *"Very truly I tell you, the Son of Man can do nothing by himself; he can do only what he sees his Father doing, because whatever the Father does the Son also does."* In John 5:30 Jesus said, *"By myself I can do nothing."*

As we read these verses we must keep in mind that Jesus possessed all the power and attributes of deity. However, He did not use them except at the pleasure of the Father. He steadfastly refused to act on His own initiative. This revealed part of the perfection of His Life, and it serves as an example for us.

Furthermore, we read the following words written by Paul in Philippians 1:3-6.

> *"I thank my God every time I remember you. In all my prayers for all of you, I always pray with joy because of your partnership in the gospel from the first day until now, being confident of this, that he who began a good work in you will carry it on to completion until the day of Christ Jesus."*

What is the *"good work"* He has promised to complete? Some believe that God's promise is to make us healthy, wealthy and wise, but Romans 8:29 gives this explanation: *"For those God foreknew he also predestined to be conformed to the likeness of his Son, that he might be the firstborn among many brothers."*

I love the way Eugene Peterson translates Romans 8:29-30 in *The Message:*

> *"God knew what he was doing from the very beginning. He decided from the outset to shape the lives of those who love him along the same lines as the life of his Son. The Son stands first in the line of humanity he restored. We see the original and intended shape of our lives there in him. After God made that decision of what his children should be like, he followed it up by calling people by name. After he called them by name, he set them on a solid basis with himself. And then, after getting them established, he stayed with them to the end, gloriously completing what he had begun."*

This is His part! This is His good work! He has brought us into His family, and He is making us like Jesus! Now, what does that mean?

I love 1 Corinthians 13, for here we find a moral picture of Jesus. I will share this with you from The Message translation:

*"If I speak with human eloquence and angelic ecstasy but don't love, I'm nothing but the creaking of a rusty gate. If I speak God's Word with power, revealing all his mysteries and making everything plain as day, and if I have faith that says to a mountain, 'Jump,' and it jumps, but I don't love, I'm nothing.*

*If I give everything I own to the poor and even go to the stake to be burned as a martyr, but I don't love, I've gotten nowhere. So, no matter what I say, what I believe, and what I do, I'm bankrupt without love.*
*Love never gives up.*
*Love cares more for others than for self.*
*Love doesn't want what it doesn't have.*
*Love doesn't strut,*
*Doesn't have a swelled head,*
*Doesn't force itself on others,*
*Doesn't revel when others grovel,*
*Takes pleasure in the flowering of truth,*
*Puts up with anything,*
*Always looks for the best,*
*Never looks back,*
*But keeps going to the end.*
*Love never dies.*

*Inspired speech will be over some day; praying in tongues will end; understanding will reach its limit. We know only a portion of the truth, and what we say about God is always incomplete. But when the Complete arrives, our incompletes will be canceled.*

> *When I was an infant at my mother's breast, I gurgled and cooed like any infant. When I grew up, I left those infant ways for good.*
>
> *We don't yet see things clearly. We're squinting in a fog, peering through a mist. But it won't be long before the weather clears and the sun shines bright! We'll see it all then, see it all as clearly as God sees us, knowing him directly just as he knows us! But for right now, until that completeness, we have three things to do to lead us toward that consummation; Trust steadily in God, hope unswervingly, love extravagantly. And the best of the three is love."*

We see that all who are the children of God will bear the likeness of Jesus. God Himself is bringing that to pass! He will accomplish it all for those who put themselves into His hands, and simply trust Him to do it.

Well, what did that mean for me? When Mark was only 6 weeks old we moved to Tulsa, Oklahoma, where James went to work six days a week completing an interstate highway. The governor of the state was scheduled to cut the ribbon to open it on the Fourth of July.

We owned a nice home in Fort Worth, Texas, but I was determined to be with James. A friend in Tulsa found a house for us to rent. She had warned me that it was not very nice, but added that it was all she could find.

"Not very nice" was a gross understatement. The ceiling in the bathroom fell into the bathtub right before we moved in. The owner of the house had died in one of the chairs in the living room, and had not been found for five days. When the doorbell rang I always wanted to answer the door by explaining that I didn't really live there. That was the scene of the testing of my faith.

So, God was to do it all for me. I couldn't be the person I wanted to be. It simply wasn't in me, but He would make me over from the inside out. That sounded good to me; and it was in Tulsa that I set out trying to figure out what that meant and how that worked.

I wanted to be peaceful and joyful, and above all things, patient. Crying babies and spilled milk and dirty diapers made me want to scream! So, every morning I started the day in prayer. "Lord, please make me a calm, patient and joyful mother today. Help me, Lord. Please help me! I can't do it Lord. I've tried. You know I've tried. Now I'm asking You to help me." Yet, day after day things got no better. Have you ever had such an experience? I still remember the day that I got up wondering what made people believe there was a God! I remember thinking that I didn't know what good a God was who didn't help me when I needed Him.

However, help was on the way. It came through my reconnecting with a couple I had grown up with in Minneapolis. They were Janet and Bob Clark. Bob was the third generation of a missionary family. He was in Tulsa preparing for a mission aviation assignment. Janet was older than I, but she and Bob had two young children, and we spent time together every week.

We would take our children to the park. She taught me to bake bread. And one day she told me that one of her favorite Bible verses was Isaiah 26:3, *"You will keep in perfect peace those whose minds are steadfast, because they trust in you."* Janet talked about how that peace played out in her own life, and before long I was working to keep my mind on the Lord rather than on my frustrations.

How did I do that? Simply by acknowledging God's presence each day. Simply by talking to Him throughout the day. "Heavenly Father, You are here with us today. You tell me in Your Word that You are with us always. Thank

You for bringing us Your peace." Within myself I began to sense a shift toward calmness, quietness and order.

The interstate highway was finished in the nick of time. On July 3 when James arrived home from work we decided we could not spend one more night in that house! We started packing. Around midnight we loaded our two sleeping babies into the car and turned south. Just as the sun broke the horizon we pulled into Fort Worth; home at last!

Back home, my struggles continued. I had tried doing, and that didn't work for me. I had tried trusting, and that seemed to help. Doing or trusting. They seemed contradictory. Was I supposed to do a little bit of doing and a little bit of trusting? Was God going to help me to transform myself? Was I supposed to accomplish change with God's help? Whatever the message, I just couldn't seem to get it right!

About the time I was contemplating these things a speaker whose name I no longer recall said something that resonated with me. He said that he had occasion to take a matter to his lawyer. The lawyer took on his cause and said to him, "I will take care of this for you." Believing his lawyer to be as good as his word, he didn't go home and try to figure out how he could tend to it himself. He didn't call the lawyer's office every morning and beg for his help. He didn't worry every day about whether or not it was being seen after. He simply walked out the door feeling that the weight of the world had fallen off his shoulders.

Whenever he thought about it he felt grateful that it was being taken care of. He had taken his problem to one who could fix it, and he had turned it over to him. He was not aware every single day of just what his lawyer was doing, but he never doubted that he was at work, whether it was being seen or not. The lawyer had begun the work, and he would complete it! This man came to understand that doing and trusting were not contradictory. Two different people were involved. One would tend to the doing, and the other would trust him for that.

In the spiritual realm, God's part is to do the thing we have entrusted to Him, and our part is to trust Him to do it. Trust is total surrender to Him, and often the sermons we hear end there. A cry goes up that this doctrine of faith encourages Christians to sit on the porch in their rocking chairs and wait for God to act on their behalf. This is attacked as being divorced from reality and unproductive; but it is our faith that clears the way for God to work.

There is probably no better example here than the picture we have of the life guard who dives in to save a drowning swimmer. The life guard's job is to do, and the drowning person's job is to trust. It is the faith of the drowning one that clears the way for the lifeguard to do his work.

God keeps that which I have committed to Him! I like the way this truth is expressed in the last part of the following verse in 2 Timothy 1:12. *"I know whom I have believed, and am convinced that he is able to guard what I have entrusted to him until that day."*

God goes to work in behalf of all that I entrust to Him. He completes everything that He begins. My part is clearly to trust. In Proverbs 3: 5-6 we read, *"Trust in the Lord with all your heart and lean not on your own understanding; in all your ways submit to him, and he will make your paths straight."*

People who find faith difficult to understand in the spiritual realm seem oblivious to the fact that we all entrust our lives daily to all sorts of people. We could not live through a single day without faith in others. Often, they are strangers to us, yet we actually place our lives in their hands. Pharmacists, bus drivers, airline pilots, doctors —

the list goes on and on. It is trust that clears the way for these people to help us.

I began to see that my lack of trust stood in God's way. I had taken my problem to Him, but I started every day by affirming my lack of faith, for every morning I begged God to help me. "Dear God, please help me today. Please be with me. Please give me strength and wisdom. Please. Please! Please!!" By "praying" in that way I was voicing my unbelief. I simply did not believe that He was answering my earlier prayers. If I kept begging, maybe He would!

However, in the meantime, God was using everything to conform me to the image of His Son; our circumstances, blessings and difficulties, financial pressure and another pregnancy that left us with three children under 4 years of age. It was becoming clear to me that the sanctification of my life was going to involve surrender and trust on my side, and acts of development on God's side. In faith, I could place my life in God's hands. Then, through a gradual process I could begin to *"grow to become in every respect the mature body of him who is the head, that is, Christ."*

Ephesians 4:14-15 expresses it this way:

*"Then we will no longer be infants, tossed back and forth by the waves, and blown here and there by every wind of teaching and by the cunning and craftiness of people in their deceitful scheming. Instead, speaking the truth in love, we will grow to become in every respect the mature body of him who is the head, that is, Christ."*

The story of the potter and the clay has often been told to illustrate this truth. This picture of God's working with His people is used by four Bible writers: Isaiah, Jeremiah, Zechariah and Paul.

> *"Yet, O Lord, you are our Father, we are the clay, you are the potter; we are all the work of your hand"* (Isaiah 64:8).
>
> *"This is the word that came to Jeremiah from the Lord; 'Go down to the potter's house, and I will give you my message.' So I went down to the potter's house, and I saw him working at the wheel. But the pot he was shaping from the clay was marred in his hands; so the potter formed it into another pot, shaping it as seemed best to him. Then the word of the Lord came to me; "O house of Israel, can I not do with you as this potter does?" declares the Lord. "Like clay in the hand of the potter, so are you in my hand, O house of Israel"* (Jeremiah 18:1-6).

The figure of the potter also appears in Zechariah 11:13 and Romans 9:21. All of these men were strong and influential in their personal thinking and in the influence they exerted on the times in which they lived.

The picture of The Potter is frightening to many. It stands as a severe picture, but finding it four times in Holy Scripture should cause us to ask what its meaning is? How does this message apply to our lives? What does it show us about how to live?

Our text is taken from Jeremiah 18:3. *"So then I went down to the potter's house, and I saw him working at the wheel."* It is easy to imagine that we are walking down a dusty road with Jeremiah, going to see the potter.

Several years ago, James and I visited a community in Elm Mott, Texas. It is called Brazos de Dios. Many special artisans ply their craft there, and we spent a lot of time in the potter's house.

Actually, the potter's house has not changed much since Jeremiah's time. If you have ever visited a potter's house you know pretty much what Jeremiah saw when he got there. He saw the potter. He saw the potter's wheel. He saw the clay.

In the potter, he saw a talented and intelligent man. In the potter's wheel, he saw the instrument by which the potter would mold the clay for a specific purpose. In the clay, he saw a material that could be molded and made into something useful.

A lump of clay was placed on the potter's wheel. The purpose the potter had in mind was to make it into a useful vessel. Now, what can I say about the clay? Was there anything it could do to help the potter? There was only one thing. It's only chance of becoming a thing of value was to submit to the pressure of the potter's hands.

Fascinated, we watched the potter knead it and break it and wet it and begin to mold it and shape it. Later he would dry it and bake it. Left to itself we could see that the clay was of very little value. It was the potter who defined its usefulness and developed its beauty. As we have already seen, Scripture points out that these elements reveal the basic and vital relationship that exists between God and man.

In The Potter, we see the authority of God. He can do whatever He wills with the clay. We also see the attitude of God. What plans, what purpose and what design does He have for the clay? We also see the ability of God to complete what He sets out to do.

The Potter places the clay upon the wheel. He places His hand on the clay, and the wheel begins to turn. Under His fingers the clay begins to change form. His attention never wavers. His eyes are riveted to the clay.

Now, we turn our attention to the wheel. We can see in it the circumstances of life. They exert pressure on us that changes us. We realize that the wheel is necessary, but once the clay has gained its final shape and form, the wheel will be flung aside. The Potter's work will be completed. The wheel is needed for a relatively short time. The potter and the clay are of the most importance.

And what do we see in the clay? It illustrates the possibilities that lie latent within us. It is pliable. It can be molded. There are many substances that cannot be shaped, but the fingers of the potter can make impressions on clay.

These are the simple lessons of the potter's house, but here we can also learn the most profound lessons about our relationship to God. I see God. I see myself. I see the circumstances of my life. God, as The Master Potter, holds a thought in His mind that no one has ever seen; but wonder of wonders, through me He can express that thought!

What principle is taught? What purpose is suggested? What person is revealed? Unless we find answers to those questions we will rebel against the whole thing. It's no wonder it can strike fear in our hearts, for the principle of surrender seems risky. The purpose lies outside our reach, and the person is sovereign.

The principle taught is the absolute sovereignty of God and the necessity of our submission to it. The potter has absolute rights over the clay. We hear so much today about our rights, but this is all about God's rights! All rights are His! Behind His rights lie His character, His patience, His tenderness and His love.

"But," I hear you say, "the clay has no will. It has no power to choose. At this point your illustration breaks down." Let's look at this carefully. Will is the power to choose within limitations. Our choices are made within the perimeter of God's permissive will. We can never escape that.

The highest exercise of our will is the choice we make as to what principle will govern it. What will drive it? What will propel it? What will push it on? We can choose what will master it. We can choose what will master us! In choosing our master we choose our final destiny.

Our wills are ours, but we can make them God's. We can literally choose to will God's will. The message of the potter's house is that of the absolute sovereignty of God, and the wisdom that would lead us voluntarily to surrender to His will.

Beyond the principle of God's sovereignty lies the purpose. We read in Jeremiah 18:3, *"I saw him working at the wheel."* This is His part. The potter has His plan for the clay. Only He can transfer His thought to the clay. The vision for the clay is His alone. The clay is ignorant of the thought, and that is as it should be. If I knew the specifics of His vision for me, I would most likely try to create it on my own. However, I can become the expression of it through surrender to the hand of the potter.

The principle alone may bring fear, but the purpose brings comfort. The Potter has a plan, and as the wheel turns the potter is working out His plan. The beauty and purpose that lies in His mind begins to take form through the clay.

This brings us face to face with one of the deepest mysteries of human life. Mankind was created to be a medium through which God can express Himself. The apostle Paul wrote, *"For we are God's handiwork, created in Christ Jesus to do good works, which God prepared in advance for us to do"* (Ephesians 2:10). The thought here of the original Greek is that we are God's work of art. The Greek holds within it the idea of a poem. We are God's poems. God's purpose is that others will see in us some of the order and beauty of His mind! Peter wrote in I Peter 2:9, *"But you are a chosen people, a royal priesthood, a holy nation, God's special possession, that you may declare the praise of him who called you out of darkness into his wonderful light."*

In us, God gains a medium through which He reveals Himself and expresses His thought. See what we have gained! The clay, left to itself lacks form and usefulness and beauty, but when it surrenders to the potter's hand it becomes useful. There is a purpose for which it was made, and now that purpose will be fully realized.

However, the principle of surrender and the promise of purpose fulfilled can still fill me with fear unless I know the Person behind the principle and the purpose. Who is the Potter? Before I can yield I must know who the Potter is.

Clearly, God is the Potter, and who is God? God is Love. We can just as accurately say that Love is God. We can say that He is righteousness and holiness and we can name a hundred characteristics that tell us who He is; but they are all gathered together in three little words. God is Love; and we can surrender to Love. As the Potter molds the clay on the wheels, His thoughts are thoughts of Love. All of the process is a process of Love.

Until we surrender to the principle taught in the Potter's house our lives will fall short. Until we trust in the purpose of the Potter we will not know the true meaning of our own lives. In the nail-scarred hands of the Potter we see His infinite Love. It is then that we can surrender to His principle and consent to His purpose.

If we choose to take the clay out of the Potter's hands we render it useless. Vessels that were marred were thrown into the potter's field. There they lay, good for nothing but to be flung aside. However, Jesus shed His blood so that He could go out into the Potter's field and pick up those broken pieces in order to put them back on the wheel and make of them a new vessel.

What is the condition of your life today? Does it lie marred or shattered in the Potter's field? Have you wondered if God is through with you? The message of this lesson is that you cannot make anything useful of yourself, but our Loving and Merciful God will put you back onto the wheel of circumstance. If you will surrender to Him, He will shape you into a vessel of honor. Your life can bear witness to the age-old story of redemption.

As we choose for ourselves a Christian life, may we begin with the Person. May we submit to the Principle; and may we discover the Purpose so that our lives will reflect the blessing, the honor, and the glory of God.

## *I Want You, Lord*

I give to You all that I am, dear Lord.
My life, all desires are Yours.
Please accept my offerings of love I pray,
And keep them forever pure.
So, all that I want will be you, Lord.
So, all that I want will be You.

## *Think on These Things*

Explain the two sides of the life of faith, our part and God's part, and how we are called to react to them.

Have you ever been confused and wondered how the two sides of faith work together? Can you recall a life experience that confronted you with this issue?

Can you explain how doing and trusting do not contradict one another?

Explain ways in which you bring God into your day.




How would you describe the principle taught at the potter's house? What does the principle require of you?




How is it that God uses mankind as a medium through which He can express Himself?

What is the promise we find there?

What is the purpose revealed there?

I think you will enjoy reading and thinking about Isaiah 64:8, Jeremiah 18:1-6, Zechariah 11:13, Romans 9:2 and Psalm 111.

# Lesson 7
## Secret Things And Revealed Things

TEXT: *"The secret things belong to the Lord our God, but the things revealed belong to us and to our children forever, that we may follow all the words of this law."*

**Deuteronomy 29:29, NIV**

Our text for this lesson is taken from Deuteronomy 29:29. In this chapter, Moses addresses the children of Israel, calling them to honor the contract they had made with God. What was the contract? It had been entered into 40 years earlier at Mount Sinai. There were many parts to it, but its purpose can be summed up in two sentences. God promised to bless the Israelites in that they would be the nation through whom He would reveal Himself to the world. In return, the Israelites promised to love God and be obedient to Him in order to receive His blessing. Deuteronomy 29 issues a call to obedience. The message is that it is not enough to know God's Word. It must be obeyed. I found our text to be a very interesting verse that contains a very big message!

In introduction let me say that as people of faith we are often confronted with many questions. There is so much in this life that we can't understand! There are so many secrets we can't unlock! There are so many questions we don't have the answers to! In fact, there is not a field that exists in which we have found all the answers.

When we narrow this down to our own lives we don't have all the answers, either. My grandmother, who lived through a lot of heartbreak and who faced mysteries of life for which she never found answers, wanted an old song sung at her funeral. You may know it: "We'll Understand It Better Bye and Bye". In her mind, one of the joys of heaven would be coming to understand the mysteries of earth.

It's not just that we have questions. It's that we tend to resent the unknowable. Throughout history, mankind has demonstrated a determination to unlock secrets and to find answers to mysteries. This has been a proper and essential aspect of human nature. It has led to enormous strides in all fields of endeavor.

We see inquisitiveness demonstrated in the smallest child. As soon as he can talk he is asking how, what and why. As that child grows, the ways in which he questions are used by God to educate him. Curiosity is literally born into us.

However, there are limits that have been set on our ability to unlock doors and fathom secrets. God Himself sets those limits. In Acts 1:7 Jesus said to His disciples, *"It is not for you to know the times or the dates the Father has set by his own authority."* There are things that are not for us to know. There will always be limits on what will be revealed to us. There will remain *"secret things that belong unto the Lord our God"* (Deuteronomy 29:29).

Now, let's review from our text the two descriptive phrases we find in verse 29. First, it speaks of *"the secret things"*, and then of *"the things that are revealed"*. We will begin our study with things revealed, and work back to the secret things.

We are starting with the revealed things, because it is the revealed things that we are first conscious of. The literal translation of the Hebrew word translated here *"revealed "*, means *"stripped naked"*. It refers to things that are fully visible; that can be touched, that can be seen and that can be experienced by our senses.

In the final analysis, everything that man knows God has revealed to him. God's revelations have unlocked laws of science, of astronomy, of mathematics - indeed laws that lie behind all things. God's revelations take many forms. They lie behind beautiful music, or great poetry or inspiring literature. We see, and know, and experience, and make use of, and are blessed by these revealed things.

On the other hand, there are the *"secret things"*. This phrase expresses the exact opposite of the *"revealed things"*. The words translated *"secret things"* can be translated *"clothed things"*. They are things that are, but that are covered so that we cannot see them, or touch them, or handle them or weigh them. There is no doubt about their existence, but they are hidden from us.

Now, let's go back to our text and take the declarations in the order in which they appear. The first declaration is, *"The secret things belong to the Lord our God."* This is saying that things that are not revealed to us are not hidden from God. They belong to Him. He is thoroughly familiar with them.

In Hebrews 4:13 we read that *"Nothing in all creation is hidden from God's sight. Everything is uncovered and laid bare before the eyes of him to whom we must give account."*

So much for the hidden things. So much for the secret things. What of the revealed things? As we have seen, the revealed things are the songs that are composed or the books that are penned or the scientific principles that are discovered. The hidden or secret thing is the thought or the process that produced the revealed things. I can sing the song, or read the book, or investigate the science. But where did these things come from? From where did they originate?

In Psalm 139:1-2 the Psalmist wrote, *"O Lord, you have searched me and you know me. You know when I sit and when I rise; you perceive my thoughts from afar."* What does that mean? Does it mean that from a far and distant place God understands my thoughts? We know that is not the meaning, because God is never far from us. *"For in Him we live and move and have our being"* (Acts 17:28). What does this mean?

It means that before my thoughts are formed and before I express them in words or action or discovery, God knows them! He understands our thoughts in the making! The things we create or discover are the revealed things, and the revealed things are ours. However, the working of the mind is hidden from view. It is a mystery, even to us, and the mystery lies with God.

*"The secret things are known to God."* This statement stabilizes our lives, for it is wonderful to rest assured that the many things in life that confuse and confound us are not things that baffle God. He holds the answers to the mysteries we are not able to solve. He knows the answers to questions we do not know how to ask. He knows! The secret things belong to Him, and He knows all things.

What does this have to do with us? Why does this matter? Why should we give it any thought? How is this part of the incredible blessing of the Christian life? What does it have to do with my life day by day?

This is important because the revealed things and the secret things are closely related. Every single revealed thing is intimately united to a secret thing. All revealed things originate within forces that are hidden.

Once we learn that the things that are revealed teach us about the things that are hidden, we will begin to see that all things every day unveil to us truths of the Son of God. Day by day things can be revealed to us that uncover the mysteries that surround us.

We often miss out on this life blessing because we begin thinking at the wrong end of things, and the way we think determines the way we experience life. We need to always begin — not with what is seen — but with God, who is not seen. This is our calling as Christians.

In his book entitled *Bread for the Journey*, Henri Nouwen writes, "When God took on flesh in Jesus Christ, the uncreated and the created, the eternal and the temporal, the divine and the human, became united. This unity meant that all that is mortal now points to the immortal, all that is finite now points to the infinite. In and through Jesus all creation has become like a splendid veil, through which the face of God is revealed to us."

What unspeakable richness this brings to our lives! All is sacred because all that is speaks of God's redeeming Love. Oceans and winds, mountains and deserts, flowers and trees, sun, moon and stars and all the animals and people are sacred windows offering us glimpses of God.

However, rather than beginning with God, people almost always begin with what can be seen, felt and experienced. We begin with our disappointments, our disillusionments, our pain, our struggles, our failures and our fears. We begin with our own personal experiences, and circumstances and self-centered perspectives. In order to have mysteries unveiled to us, we must look first to God. Above all we must first seek His perspectives, His will and His ways.

In Jeremiah 33:2-3 we read these words:

*"This is what the Lord says, he who made the earth, the Lord who formed it and established it — the Lord is his name: Call to me and I will answer you and tell you great and unsearchable things you do not know."*

What are the unsearchable things? The word used in the Hebrew language for unsearchable things refers to things that are inaccessible. The laws that lie behind the entire universe are all part of the inaccessible things. The laws of God govern every aspect of being. We live in an age that continues to discover those laws and the truths that lie behind them. The secret things belong to God. In His way and in His time, He reveals them. In Daniel 12:4 we read that knowledge will increase as we come to the end of time.

The revealed things become ours, but for what purpose? Our text for this lesson, Deuteronomy 29:29, answers that question for us. God makes us possessors of hidden things so that we can live in accordance with His laws. "That we may do all the words of this law." Taking the primary thought, we find a great truth spoken here. That truth is that everything revealed is the revelation of a law. The further revelation is that as soon as we discover and obey the law, we enter into communion with the secret thing behind it which is the intelligence, the power and the Love of God!

You may still be wondering what this means to you? Illustrations abound in virtually every realm. Electricity offers us a good example. How are our homes and buildings lighted? By means of electricity. How do we get it? People developed ways of tapping into it and of transporting it. I know very little about how it is produced or how it works, but I benefit greatly from it.

I know that in 1879 there were laws revealed to a man who was researching the physics of electricity. Using lower current electricity and a small carbonized filament, Thomas Edison developed the first practical incandescent electric light and found himself in the midst of powerful forces mankind had never dreamed of before.

Today we know that electricity can travel around the world seven times in one second! If we were to consider whether there is more electricity in a big city like Fort Worth, Texas, or in remote parts of the world, our first thought might be that it would be in Fort Worth; but that is not true. In the most remote areas on earth they have the same force of electricity that is available to us, but people in those areas have not obeyed the law and harnessed the force, and so the blessing of electricity is unavailable to them.

The principle stands firm. Always, the unseen law lies behind the revelation of the hidden things. Once you discover the law and obey it, you immediately are in touch with the infinite force that lies behind it.

Dr. Morgan writes that this is the philosophy of prayer. God is revealing Himself in everything! Everything is revealing a law of God. As we recognize it and obey it we are put in touch with the Spiritual Power that lies behind it.

How true is this? Let's consider some simple illustrations. If I take a wild rose and hold it in my hand, in looking at it, I observe the revealed thing. It has form, and color and fragrance. But there are laws that lie hidden in that rose. If I discover them, and work with them, what will happen? The secrets of the rose will be revealed to me. Then I will be able to cooperate with God in developing out of that wild rose the most gorgeous and innovative of roses.

Let us move to another realm, and go to the words of the Lord Jesus Himself. *"The wind blows, and you hear the sound."* Here are revealed things, and they belong to us. We feel the wind. We hear the sound it makes. Sometimes it blows as a gentle caress. Sometimes it is so powerful that it brings awful destruction; but the secret of the wind belongs to God. Where is the wind coming from? Where is it going?

Once I was watching the weather report. The weather man was reporting about tornadoes. Later the report followed three hurricanes across the trackless ocean. Where were these winds and storms coming from? Where would they go? With all of our modern technology, we cannot predict them exactly! Men continue to work to uncover the laws that control it all, but God holds the mighty secret of the wind.

Then, there is the mind of mankind. As scientists continue to study the brain, we are learning more about the laws that govern it. We learn of brain nerve cells, synapses, neurotransmitters and gray matter, but once the brain has died it seems that the mind lives on.

We read an example of this in Luke 16:19-31:

> "There was a rich man who was dressed in purple and fine linen and lived in luxury every day. At his gate was laid a beggar named Lazarus, covered with sores and longing to eat what fell from the rich man's table. Even the dogs came and licked his sores.
>
> The time came when the beggar died and the angels carried him to Abraham's side. The rich man also died and was buried. In Hades, where he was in torment, he looked up and saw Abraham far away, with Lazarus by his side. So he called to him, 'Father Abraham, have pity on me and send Lazarus to dip the tip of his finger in water and cool my tongue, because I am in agony in this fire.'
>
> "But Abraham replied, 'Son, remember that in your lifetime you received good things, while Lazarus received bad things, but now he is comforted here and you are in agony. And besides all this, between us and you a great chasm has been set in place, so that those who want to go from here to you cannot, nor can anyone cross over from there to us.'
>
> "He answered, 'Then I beg you, father, send Lazarus to my family, for I have five brothers. Let him warn them, so that they will not also come to this place of torment.'
>
> "Abraham replied, 'They have Moses and the Prophets; let them listen to them.'

> *'No, father Abraham,'* he said, *'but if someone from the dead goes to them, they will repent.'*
>
> *"He said to him, 'If they do not listen to Moses and the Prophets, they will not be convinced even if someone rises from the dead.'"*

What a story! How can the mind live on after death? We must simply say that the secret things belong to God.

We need to be aware that God is revealing Himself to us every single day. He reveals Himself in the sky, and birds, and storms, and through other people. If we watch, we will be taught by Him concerning the laws that exist behind everything. As we obey His law, as we live in harmony with it, our lives will progress from glory to glory, and that is of the Lord.

> *"Now the Lord is the Spirit, and where the Spirit of the Lord is, there is freedom. And we all, who with unveiled faces contemplate the Lord's glory, are being transformed into his image with ever-increasing glory, which comes from the Lord, who is the Spirit"* (2 Corinthians 3:17-18).

I have been thinking about how this works in our personal lives, and within our families. Many things are revealed every single day. The revealed things lie in the words that are spoken, in the actions that are taken, in the environment that is created, and in the circumstances that we then move into. Behind all the things that are revealed lie the things that are hidden and secret; these are the mysteries that have brought us to where we are today.

One of the most important laws is given to us in Galatians 6:7-10:

> *"Do not be deceived: God cannot be mocked. A man reaps what he sows. Whoever*

> *sows to please his flesh, from the flesh will reap destruction; whoever sows to please the Spirit, from the Spirit will reap eternal life. Let us not become weary in doing good, for at the proper time we will reap a harvest if we do not give up. Therefore, as we have opportunity, let us do good to all people, especially to those who belong to the family of believers."*

What is sown in our thoughts is reaped in our experience. In Andrew Murray's book *The Inner Life*[5] he expresses this truth in this way. "The outward form is the visible expression of the hidden inward life." The things that lie within can only be revealed to us by God Himself. No friend and no counselor can bring them to light; but we can go to God as the Psalmist did in Psalm 139:23-24. Our prayer can be, *"Search me, God, and know my heart; test me, and know my anxious thoughts. See if there is any offensive way in me. And lead me in the way everlasting."* He will honor your prayer and reveal to you the mysteries that lie within your own heart.

And then what happens? If the hidden things change, then the revealed things will change as well. When thoughts that are hidden change, things that are revealed change. When the things that are hidden change, attitudes that are revealed change. The tone of voice changes. The ways in which relationships are expressed change. God has revealed what He wants to express through us, and that is love! Hidden from sight, He can fill our hearts with His own Love, and that is what will be revealed for all to see. As love is sown, love will be reaped. As we live in accordance with God's law we become co-creators with Him.

May we learn in all things how to orient our lives to the unseen, always placing God at the center of our thinking. May we become more sensitive and aware of the ways in which He is revealing Himself to us. May we rest in the peace of knowing that He will show us all that we need to know. In so doing, may we determine to align ourselves to the laws He has established, for in this way we become One with His purposes. Then we can be used by Him to bring about the doing of His Will and the coming of His Kingdom, and we will bring honor and glory to His name. These are all blessings of the Christian Life!

I close with Romans 11:33-36:

*Oh, the depth of the riches of the wisdom and knowledge of God! How unsearchable his judgments, and his paths beyond tracing out! "Who has known the mind of the Lord? Or who has been his counselor?" "Who has ever given to God, that God should repay them?" For from him and through him and to him are all things. To him be the glory forever! Amen.*

## *Praise, Love and Honor*

You're the power in the storm.
You rule land and sea.
You author creation,
Yet You come live in me!

All praise to You, Father,
All love to Your Son
All honor, Sweet Spirit,
Our God, Three in One!

## *Think on These Things*

All of us have areas of our lives that present unanswered questions. Can you pinpoint such an area?

Explain the meaning of revealed things and hidden things.

Can you share an example from your own life of a revealed thing?

Can you share an example from your own life of a hidden thing?

How is life held fast by the knowledge that God knows all things? How does that bring you stability?

Give an example of how secret things and revealed things are united.

What does it mean to begin thinking at the wrong end of things?

Give an example of how beginning with God changes the way you experience life.




Can you give an example of how you are living out the laws of God?




Can you share how God has recently revealed to you how His laws are working?




I think you will enjoy reading and thinking about Isaiah 40:12-31.

## Lesson 8
### What Is the Secret of Jehovah?

TEXT: *"The Lord confides in those who fear Him; And he will make his covenant known to them."*

**Psalm 25:14, NIV**

Psalm 25 was written by David. I enjoy studying Scripture in many translations, but I find a special beauty and accuracy and depth in the *King James Translation*. That is the translation I am using in this lesson.

As we begin, note that Psalm 25:1-7 holds a prayer:

*"Unto thee, O Lord, do I lift up my soul. O my God, I trust in thee: let me not be ashamed, let not mine enemies triumph over me. Yea, let none that wait on thee be ashamed; let them be ashamed who transgress without cause. Show me thy ways, O Lord; teach me thy paths. Lead me in thy truth, and teach me; for thou art the God of my salvation; on thee do I wait all the day. Remember, O Lord, thy tender mercies and thy loving-kindness; for they have been ever of old. Remember not the sins of my youth, nor my transgressions; according to thy mercy remember thou me for thy goodness' sake, O Lord."*

In verses 8-10 God's goodness is recognized.

*"Good and upright is the Lord; therefore, he will teach sinners in the way. The meek will he guide in justice; and the meek will he teach his way. All the paths of the Lord are mercy and truth unto such as keep his covenant and his testimonies."*

Verse 11 is another prayer.

*"For thy name's sake, O Lord, pardon mine iniquity, for it is great."*

Note that David does not minimize his sin. Rather, he takes it to a great Savior!

Verses 12-15 offers up the testimony of David's soul to God.

*"What man is he that feareth the Lord? Him shall he teach in the way that he shall choose. His soul shall dwell at ease, and his seed shall inherit the earth. The secret of the Lord is with those who fear him, and he will show them his covenant. Mine eyes are ever toward the Lord; for he shall pluck my feet out of the net."*

Psalm 25 closes with another prayer in verses 16-22.

*"Turn unto me and have mercy upon me, for I am desolate and afflicted. The troubles of my heart are enlarged. O bring thou me out of my distresses. Look upon mine affliction and my pain, and forgive all my sins. Consider mine enemies; for they are many, and they hate me with cruel hatred. O, keep my soul, and deliver me; let me not be ashamed; for I put my trust in thee. Let integrity and uprightness preserve me; for I wait on thee. Redeem Israel, O God, out of all his troubles."*

The outstanding words found here are words of sorrow. A great wail of desolation, of affliction and of distress echoes throughout. Some of us may find ourselves in a place of sadness and grief today. That is where David was, yet as we read Psalm 25 we discover that its primary message is not of despair, but of hope and confidence. The singer is acutely aware that pressure is bearing down upon him, yet he rises above it; and his sob is transformed into a song. How does that happen? How is that possible?

We saw that Psalm 25 opens and closes with prayer. Between those two paragraphs runs a major note expressing the goodness of God. Out of that song of declaration we have taken one verse as our text for this lesson, believing it to hold the secret of song in the midst of sorrow. How can we discover the secret? *"The secret of the Lord is with them that fear Him; And He will shew them His covenant"* (Psalm 25:14).

First, we note that a blessing is mentioned here; "The secret of the Lord". The secret will be the blessing! Second, we will meditate on how we can receive the blessing. In conclusion, we will consider one of the results of the blessing.

*"The secret of the Lord"* - that phrase immediately brings to our minds the text that we studied in Lesson 7; *"The secret things belong to the Lord our God; but the things that are revealed belong to us and to our children forever"* (Deuteronomy 29:29). The first thing we need to know is that the word "secret" in today's text has an entirely different meaning from the word *"secret"* that we studied in our last lesson. The *"secret things"* that we studied in Lesson 7 were things that exist, but are hidden. Literally, they are veiled things, covered things, things which we cannot discover on our own. They are the mysteries of life; the answers we do not have; the laws of God that have not yet been revealed to us.

However, the word translated *"secret"* here is quite different. In order to correctly interpret it and to more fully understand the message hidden in it, we are going to examine four texts that all contain the same Hebrew word. In every case the Hebrew word could be translated *"secret"*. However, we will discover in each of these verses surprising variations of meaning. Putting them all together will feel like constructing a puzzle, and will give us something of the breadth and depth of meaning that lies in this familiar declaration; *"The secret of Jehovah is with them that fear Him."* We will also discover how this truth brings supernatural blessing to our lives!

First, we will turn to Psalm 111:1. It reads, "Praise ye Jehovah. I will give thanks to Jehovah with my whole heart, In the COUNCIL of the upright and in the congregation." The word "council" as it is used here refers to a group that is brought together for deliberation or advice. The reference is to a group of friends and advisers. It is an intimate word, but in no way, does it refer to a clique. Rather, there is a breadth to it that describes the people of God and the close ties of fellowship that they sustain. The Hebrew word translated "secret" in Deuteronomy 29:29, is translated "council" in Psalm 111:1! It would be absolutely accurate to read our text, "THE COUNCIL of the Lord is with those who fear Him." The fellowship of the saints is with those who fear the Lord.

Next, let us read Psalm 55:14. *"We took sweet COUNSEL together; We walked in the house of God and with the throng."* Yet another translation given to our Hebrew word is "counsel", and it holds a different suggestion. To counsel is to give advice or instruction. It is an accurate translation to state that "THE COUNSEL (the advice and instruction) of Jehovah is with them that fear Him."

Now, let us turn to Proverbs 3:32. *"The perverse is an abomination to the Lord; But His friendship is with the upright."* Here we find yet another accurate translation for our Hebrew word. Our text could accurately be translated, "THE FRIENDSHIP of Jehovah is with them that fear Him."

Now, we are going to go back and examine these three verses again. Remember that WE ARE NOT CONSIDERING WHAT THESE VERSES ARE SAYING, but how the verses use the Hebrew word translated "secret". We want to delve into the depths of what David meant when he said, "THE SECRET of the Lord is with them that fear Him."

In the first verse we considered, the psalmist wrote of "the council of the upright". Here David used our word in its simplest sense. This translation takes the word "secret" back to its root idea. That idea is of a group of people who have gathered together sharing common belief. They are of one mind and heart. They have a single purpose. They are in complete agreement. This is a beautiful idea, and one that is seldom realized. We know of at least one time in the history of humanity when there was such a gathering, and it was on the Day of Pentecost. The idea contained in this Hebrew word is perfect unity and total harmony, because Jehovah sits on the council, and there is no controversy between those on the council and Him.

However, there is more included in this translation. It suggests the awareness of perfect friendship, even if no word is spoken at all. It is a friendship that does not demand conversation, but is equal to absolute silence.

For the sake of illustration, let's turn our thoughts toward the friendships in our own lives. We all have many acquaintances, but just a few friends, and there are not many that we feel safe and comfortable being absolutely silent with.

I have always been able to mark the moment in time when silence became part of the friendship my husband, James, and I share. Shortly after our youngest left for Baylor, James and I struck out one evening to take a walk. I was talking, talking, talking, and suddenly James stopped walking and he said, "Honey. Honey. Now that our children are gone you do not have to fill every minute with conversation. You are wearing me out! May we just walk along quietly?"

I don't know how you would have responded, but I was amazed to discover how relieved I was! I had not realized what I was doing, but when he put it into words, I knew I had accepted that as my responsibility. Now that our children were gone, I was to keep the conversation going!

Now there is a lot of silence in our home. It is sweet and restful and peaceful, and we like it! There is no need for a lot of words. There is mutual understanding. There is usually no controversy. Nothing is hidden. It is a silence that is filled to overflowing with joy and peace and love.

This is part of THE SECRET of God. It is a secret He longs to reveal to us. It is a secret He longs to share with us. It is A FRIENDSHIP that is serene and calm and dignified, a friendship in which it is safe to be silent, a friendship in which there is no need for speech.

This is the first thought; the council of the upright, the assembly of the upright. It is the meeting and the sitting together in one mind and heart and spirit. Mark this well; the very idea of speech is not in the word "secret" or "council" as it is used here. It is important to under-stand that!

We have seen a different suggestion in Psalm 55:14. "We took sweet COUNSEL together." Note that the silence is broken. There is speech here, but it is the speech of everyday conversation. As our word is used here it suggests the sweet freedom that comes when friends understand each other, and when the words we speak do not have to be measured.

There is a familiar passage on friendship that was authored by Dinah Maria Muloch Craik (1826-1887). It appeared in her book *A Life for a Life* published in 1859.

"Oh, the joy,
The inexpressible delight of being alone
with your friend
when you can pour out everything that is
in your soul, all you think,
wheat and chaff together, knowing that
your listening friend will with the breath
of kindness blow away the chaff and keep
only the grain."

Out of the capacity for silence comes this kind of speech. "We took sweet counsel together." We talked to each other, and we said all that was in our hearts. This is the glad freedom that is experienced when friends understand one another.

The secret of the Lord is with those who have no secrets from Him. The secret of the Lord is with those who pour out their hearts before Him, and who listen so that God can talk to them of what is in His heart as He reveals His will, and His purpose.

Can God speak freely to each of us? There are those who say that God no longer speaks as He did long ago. I would say that the measure to which He fails to communicate with us is the measure to which we fail to communicate with Him.

Recently I was talking with a young girl who said, "Every time I read my Bible, God speaks to me. My thoughts are clearer. My goals come into focus. My spirit is strengthened." Friendship with God involves being able to pour everything out to Him. Then He can speak freely to us.

Now we will turn to Proverbs 3:32. Once again we want to discover how the word translated "secret" is used. *"The perverse is an abomination to the Lord: But HIS SECRET is with the upright."* What thought is being conveyed here? Here we do not find the silence. Here we do not find confidential speech about private matters, and the give and take of conversation about the deepest of things. Here the thought is of receiving advice and guidance. To those that fear Him, the Lord can give guidance and advice. From behind them He can say, *"This is the way: walk ye in it"* (Isaiah 30:21).

There is one more place in the Bible where our Hebrew word translated "secret" appears. Proverbs 11:13 says, *"A talebearer revealeth **"secrets.**"* This seems to have the least to do with our theme, but here our word is used in its fullest sense. What are secrets? They are a sign of friendship. They are the special confidences of friendship. They demonstrate that two people trust one another enough to share their hearts.

God can tell His secrets to some people. He can share special confidences with them. In Genesis 18:17 He said, "Shall I hide from Abraham that thing which I do?" God did not hide from Abraham that He was going to destroy Sodom and Gomorrah. Lot knew nothing of it, but Abraham, the man of faith, received the secret of the Lord. And God still reveals to us His secrets. He will share with us the depths of His heart. He will open up to us the truth of His purposes.

Often, we find that we cannot share those secrets with others. People in the Bible told of receiving from God secrets they could not share. Paul wrote:

> "I knew a man in Christ, fourteen years ago (whether in the body, I know not; or whether out of the body, I know not; God knows, such a one caught up even to the third heaven . . . and I heard unspeakable words, which it is not lawful for a man to utter"
> (2 Corinthians 12:2-4).

God told Paul secrets, and to this day we do not know what they were; but they made him the man he became.

God's secrets are not revealed to the world through the telling of them, but through the living of them. The secrets are revealed through the lives that have been changed to bring honor and glory to His name.

Here we see that our puzzle has almost fallen into place. We have found four things to remember about one Hebrew word that is translated "SECRETS".

First, there is the thought of sitting in peaceful silence and of having no need for words because there is no controversy.

Second, is the thought of mutual, easy conversation in which words do not have to be measured because they will be understood. It is the picture of just two people engaged in intimate conversation.

Third, there is the thought of receiving advice, and counsel and guidance.

Fourth, there are special confidences in which God reveals to us what He is going to do. All of these meanings are bound up in the Hebrew word that is translated "secret" in our text. "The SECRET of the Lord is with them that fear Him."

Let us go back to Psalm 25. Here, David said everything. He poured out his desolation and sorrow. When he stood in the presence of God, he did not play the hypocrite. When he felt rebellion, he expressed it. He never pretended resignation. He never pretended acceptance when he was filled with anger and confusion. We need to be honest with God, and to remember that our honesty never makes God angry.

Don't we all long for *"the secret of the Lord"*? Just to be able to sit in silence with Him. Just to talk to Him and to know that He hears me, and that He talks back to me. Just to have His guidance and direction, and perhaps to one day have Him tell me what He is going to do. These things make up the blessing of *"the secret of the Lord"*.

Before we move on we need to notice another word. Every place in Psalm 25 where the word "Lord" appears, the actual Hebrew word is "Jehovah". If the word "Adoni" were used, it would suggest God's sovereignty. If the word "Elohim" were used, it would suggest His might, but Jehovah suggests his adaptability. In all our needs and all our sorrows, in every circumstance, He becomes to each one of us exactly what we need. He adapts Himself to meet our needs and our capacity for understanding.

Who is given the *"secret"* of the Lord? There is a condition given here. It is with *"those who fear Him"*. What does it mean to fear God? There are two kinds of fear. There is the fear that God will hurt me, "servile" fear; and there is the fear that I will grieve God, "filial" fear. This last kind of fear is the kind that Psalm 25 refers to.

These two fears stand in diametric opposition to each other. "Servile" fear lives in constant dread of God. Out of that kind of fear comes bitterness, confusion, and even hatred. But what of the "felial" fear? What comes out of it? Proverbs 8:13 tells us that *"The fear of the Lord is to hate evil."* Proverbs 16:6 tells us that *"By the fear of the Lord men depart from evil."* It is true that the secret of Jehovah cannot be given to people who enjoy and cling to their sin. The secret of Jehovah is given to those who long to please God; to those who do not want to bring grief to Him. It is given to those who love what God loves and hate what God hates.

Many of you know the *"secret"* of the Lord. You sit with Him quietly. You carry on familiar and comfortable conversations with Him. You receive His wisdom and guidance, and He may have shared with you His secrets. But if that has not been true for you, I pray that you will stop now and consider that carefully. God waits for us. He waits for us to be ready to receive the blessing of His secrets. He waits for us to turn from our ways to seek His ways. It is our own ways that make it impossible for us to discover the secrets of God, even though we live in the very middle of them. The secret of Jehovah is that we can have an intimate and personal friendship with a living God, but He cannot give Himself to those who love evil; or to those who love themselves and their ways more than they love Him.

Then we have one final word. What is the result of this wonderful blessing? *"He will show them His covenant."* Psalm 25:14. What is a covenant? It is an agreement that is entered into. When Psalm 25 was written, it was a covenant of law. Today it is a covenant of grace that God enters into with us through His Son. The old prophet in Jeremiah described this great and gracious covenant.

> *"This is the covenant that I will make with the house of Israel. I will put my law in their inward parts, and in their heart will I write it; and I will be their God, and they shall be my people; and they shall teach no more every man his neighbor, and every man his brother, saying, Know the Lord; for they shall all know Me, from the least of them unto the greatest of them, saith the Lord; for I will forgive their iniquity, and their sin will I remember no more"* (Jeremiah 31:33).

The first application of this promise was to the house of Israel. However, the principle within it is an agreement that God enters into with all of His people. He enters the agreement with those who hate evil and turn from it by finding their way to Jesus Christ. This is one of the great blessings of the Christian life.

*"He will show them His covenant."* The thought here in Psalm 25:14 is not that He will make plain to us the terms of the covenant so we can understand it. The thought is that

we shall see the covenant fulfilled in the experience of our own lives.

To have His *"secret"* is the fear of the Lord, and what grows out of that? Through all the paths along which our lives take us we will watch and will see the faithfulness of God's covenant with us. Be assured that there will be days, dark and mysterious, when all will seem to be working against us. Along with Jacob we may find ourselves saying, "All these things are against me." But come forward just a little way and you will find yourself saying with Jacob, "The God of the covenant has been with me all of my days."

Those who have known Him the longest can trace the strange paths down which they have traveled. There have been hours of agony and hours of deliverance. There have been nights sailing storm-tossed seas when we have heard through the gloaming His dear voice; "It is I. Do not be afraid." He is always showing us His covenant, and He will continue to do so. Whatever our situation is today, whatever tomorrow holds, may our present consciousness be always of God, for it is in the awareness of His presence that our sorrow is transformed into our song of His salvation. This stands as one of the great blessings of the Christian life!

## A Song of Victory

A song of victory,
a song of praise.
Hearts filled with thanksgiving
to You we raise.
Our God, we exalt You;
Your anthem we raise.
You're our song, our salvation,
The ancient of days.

With unfailing Love, You lead us
As those who've been redeemed.
With Your great hand, You guide us
In paths that are yet unseen.
Who among gods is like You, my Lord?
Who among gods is like You?
Majestic and holy; Awesome and mighty;
Who works wonders for me and for you.

In faithfulness lead us all of our days,
May we inherit Your grace.
Prepare for us a dwelling, O Lord.
Lead us safely to that place.

# *Think on These Things*

Can you compose a prayer of your own using the petition found in Psalm 25:1-7 as a pattern?

Do you believe that blessing travels with sorrow? How have you experienced such a time?

How can our sobs be transformed into songs?

Using our four references, outline the Secret of Jehovah as we find it revealed here. Include the blessing that is found at each point.

Can you share a recent experience of God speaking to you?

What is the significance of the word *"Jehovah"*?

What are the two kinds of fear we found in this lesson?

How does God reveal to us His covenant?

How do you remain aware of God's presence?

I think you will enjoy reading and thinking about Psalm 28.

# Lesson 9

## Jubilation in Desolation

TEXT: *"Though the fig tree does not bud, and there are no grapes on the vines, though the olive crop fails and the fields produce no food, though there are no sheep in the pen and no cattle in the stalls, yet I will rejoice in the Lord, I will be joyful in God My Savior."*

**Habakkuk 3:17-18, NIV**

Our text is one of the best-known in all of Scripture about the blessing of praise and thanksgiving in all things! It captures our attention with its rhythm and movement, and with the contrast that exists between the conditions that are described and the experience that is claimed.

The first part of the text, Habakkuk 3:17-18, lays out a picture of desolation, but it only serves as an introduction to the radiant jubilation that follows. Dr. Morgan points out that the conditions can be described as *"desolation"*, and the experience can be described as *"jubilation"*. Our first response on reading this might be to ask, "Was this man, Habakkuk, crazy or deluded or a fanatic? How could he look upon such desolation and experience jubilation?"

To find our answer we must go back to the beginning of this prophecy, and we discover that this triumphant way of looking at the situation was not where Habakkuk began.

Listen to his words in Habakkuk 1:2-4:

*"How long, Lord, must I call for help, but you do not listen? Or cry out to you, "Violence!", but you do not save? Why do you make me look at injustice? Why do you tolerate wrongdoing? Destruction and violence are*

*before me; there is strife, and conflict abounds. Therefore, the law is paralyzed, and justice never prevails. The wicked hem in the righteous, so that justice is perverted."*

When Habakkuk looked around him he saw anarchy, political disorder and chaos. There was no justice, no fair-ness, no righteousness. He was overwhelmed by the iniquity of his time. Such is the history of mankind. Such is history as it is being written today. What did Habakkuk do?

First, we see that he was absolutely honest with God. He voiced his doubt and fear. There are times in life that would lead us to question God, and that always bring despair and confusion. Habakkuk acknowledged that was where he was. Job provides us with an example of a man who refused to go there. However, if we allow ourselves to move down that road, we surely do not want to stay there.

What changed Habakkuk's tune? What brought him to a strong new place of confidence? The answer to this question is very interesting. We find our first clue at the beginning of Habakkuk 3. Note how the chapter is designated; *"A prayer of Habakkuk the prophet."* Then we encounter our first clue. It is found in a strange, unusual and mystical word, *"Shigionoth"*. There have been many opinions as to what this word means. The notes in my Bible state that this is a word of "uncertain meaning". There is only one other place that this word appears in the Bible. It appears over Psalm 7. There we find it in the singular form; *"shiggaion"*. In Habakkuk, it appears in the plural form.

Translators have found some agreement in defining the words of Psalm 7 as poetry that is almost incoherent. They struggled with what seemed to be loud cries of pain and anguish. It seems that Psalm 7 records the cries of a man who lived through great trials and had come to a place of deliverance. In Chapter 3 of Habakkuk, we find this same kind of cry. It is a cry of anguish that defies translation. It is a cry of brutal honesty. It is the cry of a heart laid bare.

There is one time that stands out in my mind when I heard such a cry, and I have never forgotten it. James and I had not been married long when his Uncle Royce died. We went to the funeral, and then to the cemetery. Royce's wife, James' Aunt Cordie, was standing by the grave. When they started lowering the casket into the ground a mighty groan came from her, and then she cried out, "Tell me this isn't so. Oh, someone tell me this isn't so!" It was a cry expressing great suffering.

Let's stop here and look at our own lives. I'm quite certain that no one has ever lived who has not at some time been brought to this place of mental, emotional and spiritual pain; and when you are there, the cries of your heart defy translation. What brought you to that place? Are you there now, or have you experienced deliverance? The answers to those questions will determine how you hear the rest of this lesson. Hold those thoughts as we return to *Habakkuk*.

First, Habakkuk cries out to God, *"Lord, I have heard of your fame; I stand in awe of your deeds, Lord. Repeat them in our day, in our time make them known"* (Habakkuk 3:2). Notice that his cry is not "Save me, give me, do for me". Rather it is "Keep your work alive. Complete it. Accomplish Your plans."

God answered that cry. In the stillness of Habakkuk's own soul, God answered him. In the stillness of His soul! How many of us have learned to be still and quiet in our own souls? When we don't understand, can we wait with quiet faith, with genuine excitement, with aggressive expectation listening for God's voice? And what God said to Habakkuk is what He says to us!

We read God's answer beginning in Habakkuk 1:5: *"Look at the nations and watch - and be utterly amazed. For I* am going to do something in your days that you would not believe even if you were told."

The first part of God's answer stands firm as His answer to mankind's cries of anguish and to our personal cries. "Look, and watch, for I am going to do something in your days that you would not believe even if you were told."

In Habakkuk 1:6-11, God tells Habakkuk what He is going to do:

"I am raising up the Babylonians, that ruthless and impetuous people who sweep across the whole earth to seize dwelling places not their own. They are a feared and dreaded people; they are a law to themselves and promote their own honor. Their horses are swifter than leopards, fiercer than wolves at dusk. Their cavalry gallops headlong; their horsemen come from afar. They fly like an eagle swooping to devour; they all come intent on violence. Their hordes advance like a desert wind and gather prisoners like sand. They mock kings and scoff at rulers. They laugh at all fortified cities; by building earthen ramps they capture them. Then they sweep past like the wind and go on — guilty people, whose own strength is their god."

In Habakkuk 1:12 we pick up on Habakkuk's astonishment and on his honest confusion. He engages in an argument with God. "Lord, are you not from everlasting? My God, my Holy One, you will never die. You Lord, have appointed them to execute judgment; you, my Rock, have ordained them to punish." In effect Habakkuk is saying, "God, how can You?"

Then we move down to Habakkuk 2:1: "I will stand at my watch and station myself on the ramparts; I will look to see what he will say to me, and what answer I am to give to this complaint."

In the Old Testament, the prophets often used the figure of the watchman and the watchtower to express an attitude of expectation. In *Jeremiah 6:16-17* we read, *"This is what the Lord says: "Stand at the crossroads and look; ask for the ancient paths, ask where the good way is, and walk in it, and you will find rest for your souls."*

Isaiah 21:8 reads, And the lookout shouted, *"Day after day, my lord, I stand on the watchtower; every night I stay at my post."*

Every one of us has our own watch to keep. Every one of us has our own post to man. I cannot keep your watch, and you cannot keep mine. The call goes out for us to be faithful in accepting our assignment and in manning our post!

It was while Habakkuk stayed at his post, it was while he was waiting, that God gave him the principle of all life. *"The righteous shall live by faith."* We will read from Habakkuk 2:2-4. *"Then the Lord replied: 'Write down the revelation, and make it plain on tablets so that a herald may run with it. For the revelation awaits an appointed time; it speaks of the end and will not prove false. Though it linger, wait for it; it will certainly come and will not delay. See, he is puffed up; his desires are not upright — but the righteous will live by his faithfulness.'"*

It often seems that evil and injustice hold the upper hand, but God's Word to Habakkuk is also His Word to us. Be patient, for in the fullness of My time I will work out My plans; and your part is to live by faith.

This was the point of Habakkuk's triumph over the circumstances of desolation. He could honestly say, "God, I don't understand Your ways. I don't understand Your methods. You have told me what You are going to do and I still don't understand, but my prayer is that You will keep alive Your work and will accomplish all that You have planned."

There follows in Habakkuk 3:1-19 a great psalm of worship. I will leave that for you to read on your own, but immediately following that Habakkuk looks once again at the desolation. This is written in the future tense. Habakkuk describes what is to come. Let us read his words again here in Habakkuk 3:17-18. *"Though the fig tree does not bud and there are no grapes on the vines, though the olive crop fails, and the fields produce no food, though there are no sheep in the pen and no cattle in the stalls, yet I will rejoice in the Lord, I will be joyful in God my Savior."* This is a song of higher wisdom. This singer possesses the true secret of life!

How could he dare rejoice? What was the source of his confidence? First, he knew that if all were destroyed, God could create anew. It is no secret what God can do! Habakkuk saw God as the One who could make the desert blossom like a rose. He saw God as the One who could bring low the highest mountains of difficulty. He saw God as the One who can lift us out of the deepest valleys of life. This is what any of us can see when we resolutely take our eyes off the circumstances and place them on God. In Deuteronomy 7:9, we read this promise of God's faithfulness. *"Know therefore that the Lord your God is God; he is the faithful God, keeping his covenant of love to a thousand generations of those who love him and keep his commandments."*

Next, Habakkuk knew that God's supply is unlimited. God can provide our needs by drawing on resources we know nothing of. Habakkuk knew that when all we know to do has been done and it has all come to nought, God will supply our need. Habakkuk remembered the quail and the manna in the wilderness in Numbers 11:1-35. He remembered that water had gushed forth from a rock in Exodus 17:5-6. He remembered that ravens brought Elijah bread in I Kings 17:2-3. In his heart, he knew that God supplies our needs by drawing on resources we know nothing of, and through his faith this song was formed in his heart. What do we need to remember? We need to remember what God has brought us through.

Habakkuk also knew that God could multiply little to make it last as long as was needed. He knew that during the wilderness experience the shoes of the Israelites did not wear out (Deuteronomy 29:5). He knew of the widow whose meal and oil had lasted until her need had passed (I Kings 17:7-16). He might also have argued that even if God did not create something new, if he did not supply needs from unknown sources, if He didn't make little last until distress had passed, then, if necessary, God could sustain man without food! Habakkuk could give you examples. He would remember that Moses was sustained for 40 days on the mountain (Exodus 24:12-18). He would not say that these were ordinary methods of God. Faith does not declare what will likely happen; but faith never forgets that with God all things are absolutely possible. Habakkuk sang his song of thanksgiving and praise and that kept his emphasis always on God.

This was not all that inspired Habakkuk's song. In the end, he knew that if all other things should fail, God could not fail. Only a short time before this same man had believed God to be indifferent, uncaring and inactive. Through honest communication with God he had discovered that in spite of how things looked, God was at work and He was in control! In this great song, he declared joy and peace and fullness of life even in the face of the loss of all material support. His song, resonating above the desolation of his circumstances, proclaimed Job's philosophy of faith. *"Though he slay me, yet will I hope in him"* (Job 13:15).

It is a great testimony of faith. Faith produces joy! Let us look at the joy it produced. *"I will rejoice in the Lord, I will be joyful in God my Savior"* (Habakkuk 3:18). Let everyone of us examine our own hearts. How well do we really know God? If we know Him, we will have complete confidence in Him. It is the security born out of that confidence that produces joy, and it is through that joy that we discover our strength. Nehemiah 8:10 reminds us that *"the joy of the Lord is your strength"*. In the privacy of your inner life are you filled with joy?

The words used here are remarkable! Translated literally, the Hebrew word translated "rejoice" means, "I will jump for joy in the Lord." The word translated "joyful" means "I will spin around in God my Savior." These words describe abounding joy, exuberant joy! This is what is meant by offering thanksgiving in all things. This is what is meant by offering sacrifices of praise. Everything is gone, yet I will jump for joy in Jehovah. I will spin round with delight in the God of my salvation.

What do we know of such praise in the midst of desolation? We're not talking here of praise when all is prospering, but of praise and thanksgiving that overflows in the face of calamitous failure everywhere. Habakkuk spoke out of the joy that sprang up in him. It wasn't imitation joy. It was genuine joy that filled him with jubilation in the midst of desolation! Such was the nature of his joy.

Let us turn our attention to the sphere of joy. What defines the area in which the joy exists? We look back at our verse, Habakkuk 3:18, and we read, *"I will rejoice in the Lord, I will be joyful in God My Savior."* My joy is not in what is seen. It is not joy in the circumstances. It is joy over the circumstances. I rejoice in what faith alone can comprehend. My joy lies in the realm of the unseen. If we keep looking at the realm of the seen we will be filled with sorrow and sadness, with depression and doubt. It is only through faith in God that we triumph over our circumstances.

In review, how did Habakkuk come from a position of despair to one of exuberant joy? The prophecy reveals the process. First, he was honest about his doubt; honest, not only with God, but also with himself. I'm quite sure that most who are reading this book would claim faith in God. Sometimes we are amazed to come to the realization that we are not trusting Him at all. We either trust Him in all, or we do not trust Him at all. There is no middle ground. There is no way to straddle the line. We are on either one side or the other. The degree of our joy will reflect the degree of our trust. The absence of joy will reflect the absence of trust.

Second, it was through the trials that Habakkuk found his way to higher ground. In Habakkuk 3:19 we read his testimony of faith: *"The Sovereign Lord is my strength; he makes my feet like the feet of a deer, he enables me to go on the heights."*

Habakkuk knew that the Chaldeans were coming. They would sweep over the country, leaving nothing but desolation; yet knowing what was coming, he saw that God was acting although he didn't understand His actions. That led him to the most difficult thing of all. He took his stand on the side of faith, and he waited. He took his stand, and throughout the long trial, he waited. *"I will stand upon my watch . . . I will look to see what he will say to me"* (Habakkuk 2:1).

What is happening in your life today? This is your watch! Where have you taken your stand? How are you living it out day by day? What do your children and grandchildren, your family and your friends see taking place on your watch? How do they see you living through the things that you don't understand or have answers for?

Sometimes the simplest commands of Scripture are the most difficult to obey. What about one of our favorites? *"Be still, and know that I am God"* (Psalm 46:10). It sounds so simple, but it can be the hardest thing ever! It is an exercise of faith to wait patiently for God. That is what Habakkuk did. He did not only wait. He waited and he watched and he listened; and God came to him. He came to strengthen him throughout the process of his waiting, and He came to give him a secret that would enable him to wait. Let's read again what God said in Habakkuk 2:2-4:

> *"Write down the revelation and make it plain on tablets so that a herald may run with it. For the revelation awaits an appointed time; it speaks of the end and will not prove false. Though it linger, wait for it; it will certainly come and it will not delay. See, the enemy is puffed up; his desires are not upright — but the righteous person will live by his faithfulness."*

To this waiting man God revealed this great secret; actually, the secret of all secrets. The righteous shall live by faith.

What God said to Habakkuk, he says to us. Take this principle, Habakkuk, and apply it to everything that puzzles or confounds you. The Chaldeans are coming in their pride, but I will make their wrath to praise Me. As for you, make faith in God the principle of your life; and that faith will be lived out in outrageous and joyous praise to God.

As soon as the word was spoken, Habakkuk answered it. The only explanation he had received was that God was over all. His situation had not changed. His questions had not been answered. His condition had not improved, but his song, loud cries of rejoicing, was the revelation that he had heard what God had whispered to his soul. He had allowed God to take hold of him, and he had taken hold of God.

This is an Old Testament story about an Old Testament prophet. It confirms to us that the great principle here revealed abides, and is only made more certain through the coming of the Lord Jesus Christ. Let's turn to the words of Paul in Romans 1:16-17:

> "For I am not ashamed of the gospel, because it is the power of God that brings salvation to everyone who believes: first to the Jew, then to the Gentile. For in the gospel the righteousness of God is revealed — a righteousness that is by faith from first to last, just as it is written: 'The righteous will live by faith.'"

In closing, let us consider our own situations. Do we really believe that if all we depend on were swept away, our God is able to create for our sustenance? Do we really believe He can meet our needs out of resources we know nothing of? Do we really believe that He can, if necessary, sustain life without bread? If all fails, and if in its failing we were to die, do we believe that God can never fail and is with us always? Do we really believe that God is always faithful? We will know that those beliefs have become our own when we can bring back to God the praise and thanksgiving in all things that He places in the hearts of all who trust Him.

Does this actually apply in a practical way to our lives today? This I know. Many people in our country and around the world are in real need. They don't know how they are going to make it through this day, or through tomorrow. What are they to do?

In Matthew 6:25-34 Jesus teaches us about just such times. Hear His words!

> "Therefore, I tell you, do not worry about your life, what you will eat or drink; or about your body, what you will wear. Is not life more important than food, and the body more important than clothes? Look at the birds of the air; they do not sow or reap or store away in barns, and yet your heavenly Father feeds them. Are you not much more valuable than they? Can any one of you by worrying add a single hour to your life?

> *And why do you worry about clothes? See how the lilies of the field grow. They do not labor or spin. Yet I tell you that even Solomon in all his splendor was not dressed like one of these. If that is how God clothes the grass of the field, which is here today and tomorrow is thrown into the fire, will he not much more clothe you, you of little faith? So do not worry, saying, 'What shall we eat?' or 'What shall we drink?' or 'What shall we wear?' For the pagans run after all these things, and your heavenly Father knows that you need them. But seek first his kingdom and his righteousness, and all these things will be given to you as well. Therefore, do not worry about tomorrow, for tomorrow will worry about itself. Each day has enough trouble of its own."*

Many people bear witness to the faithfulness of God. I have a friend who has found unusual success as an adult, but she grew up in a situation of financial uncertainty. Her father was an independent minister. He was not educated for this calling, and he pastored small churches. His family subsisted on what was deposited in a box at the door as his congregation departed on Sunday mornings.

Once I asked my friend how it had affected her to grow up in that way? Her answer surprised me. She said it had been a great blessing! Sometimes her family did not have any idea where their next meal was coming from, but not one time had God's provision failed them. Sometimes food would be left at their door, or an unexpected donation would arrive. She grew up knowing beyond a shadow of a doubt that God is always faithful. This is her testimony! There were years of living that way, and God was always faithful!

What is the value of all this? We can know that *"Jesus Christ is the same yesterday and today and forever"* (Hebrews 13:8). Our joy will be in proportion to our trust. Our trust will be in proportion to our knowledge of God. To know Him is to trust Him. May we be led into fuller knowledge and so find fuller faith and so enter into fuller joy.

>May we be able to truthfully sing:
>Though vine nor fig-tree neither
>Their wonted fruit shall bear:
>Though all the fields should wither,
>Nor flocks nor herds be there;
>Yet God the same abiding,
>His praise shall tune my voice;
>For while in Him abiding,
>I cannot but rejoice.

# How Majestic Is Your Name
## *Adapted from Psalm 8*

O Lord, our Lord,
How majestic is Your name in all the earth.
How majestic is Your name in all the earth!
Who has set Your glory above the heavens?
How majestic is Your name in all the earth!

You are my Lord.
You are my God.
You are my Strength and my Deliverer.
You are my Lord;
You are my God.
You are the strength of my life!

O Lord, my Lord,
How majestic is Your name in all the earth.

# *Think on These Things*

We saw that the Book of Habakkuk began with a great lament. Can you describe a time in your life when you felt that way?

What was the first step Habakkuk took toward re-establishing his confidence in God?

What was the second step?

What was God's answer to Habakkuk's questions?

What watch are you on today?

What assignment have you been given?

What was Habakkuk's prayer?

Name the things that Habakkuk remembered. How did remembering increase his faith?

List at least three things you remember God doing for you.

What produces in us the joy of the Lord?

What is the nature and the environment of that joy?

What did God tell Habakkuk to do?

Habakkuk's circumstances had not changed, but Habakkuk had changed. Describe what had happened to him.

What will you take from this lesson for your own life?

I think you will enjoy reading and thinking about Psalm 27.

# Lesson 10

## He Never Changes

TEXT: *"Jesus Christ is the same yesterday and today and forever."*

***Hebrews 13:8, NIV***

There is nothing more certain in life than is the certainty of change. As we turn the pages on our calendars we confront the passage of time, and we realize that things are changing. Recently James and I became acutely aware of change. The phone rang, and a friend had experienced a stroke. The phone rang, and we learned that another friend had died. Our neighbor, who has lived next door for almost 40 years, is moving. Our great grandson, Daniel, is walking! Daniel is talking! Personally, socially, religiously, politically, everywhere there is change.

Then we realized that we ourselves are changing. Not long ago we received a call from an old friend. We were young together. He lived through a divorce, and never remarried. For years now he has lived almost in seclusion, but every now and then he calls to check on us.

Upon hearing his voice, I said, "Jim! How in the world are you?" His unexpected response was, "I'm just sitting over here waiting to die!" I said, "Well, I guess you've joined the crowd. Isn't that what we are all doing?" Standing in the midst of change, we are all changing!

Change is the nature of life itself; but change of any kind is stressful. It is surprising that happy events are known to be just as stressful as unhappy events, for change is unsettling. What is changing for you? How is that affecting your inner reality? Change shakes us, and sometimes it shatters us. In the midst of all the changes that life brings we find ourselves longing for a center that is permanent. Indeed, in order to live lives of order and beauty we must have a foundation to build on that will last. Where can we find it?

It is not only permanence we seek, but something beyond that; the secret of growth and development, and the secret of a freshness that surprises and delights the spirit. What is it that brings the beauty of Jesus into our daily lives? We look within ourselves, and often we cannot find there the stability, the strength and the hope we desire. We turn to friends, and often we feel that on every side we encounter stories of tragedy. We look to our circumstances, and they hold uncertainty.

We may look for people who seem to model lives of beauty and order — lives that are full of life and of fresh, new perspectives and of goals attained. We may think for a while that we have found what we are seeking in a pastor or a Bible study leader. We may be inspired and energized at a spiritual retreat. However, in time we see that the people we looked to are caught up in change, just as we are. At times, we have all found ourselves crying out, "Great God! Where am I? Where am I, and which way am I to turn? To whom can I go?"

Two months before his death, Henry Francis Lyte wrote a great hymn for all humanity. It reflected his own experience as he drew ever nearer to the end of his life. Ultimate change was approaching quickly.

> Abide with me! Fast falls the eventide;
> The darkness deepens; Lord, with me abide!
> When other helpers fail, and comforts flee,
> Help of the helpless, O abide with me.
>
> Swift to its close ebbs out life's little day!
> Earth's joys grow dim; its glories pass away.
> Change and decay in all around I see,

O Thou who changest not, abide with me!

It is no wonder that this hymn is sung all over the world. I think of a story Mother told us. She and Aunt Jettie were with a group that was walking down a street in Seoul, Korea, about dusk one Sunday evening. Mother was profoundly touched to hear this song being sung in Korean, its familiar melody being wafted through open church windows onto the evening air.

How did this man come to write this hymn? It was born out of his faith, his belief, his trust, not in a philosophy or a creed or a religion, but in a person, "Jesus Christ, the One who is the same yesterday and today and forever" (Hebrews 13:8). The secret is that there is One who is unchanging. It is in Him that we find the perfect answer to the heart cry of every human being.

Sometimes as we consider spiritual things we have been exhorted to seek an anchor that will hold. An anchor belongs to a ship, and its purpose is to limit the movement of the ship. The ship tugs on the anchor. The ship would move away from the safety of the shore and out into the trackless sea, but the anchor holds it fast. The anchor provides stability.

God's promises are the same yesterday, today, and forever. They serve as an anchor for our souls. God gave His Word when He wanted to back His promises. He gave His Word, and that is a rock-solid guarantee! His Word cannot change, and His promises cannot change either.

Hebrews 6:19 gives us something to think about. *"We have this hope* (these promises) *as an anchor for the soul, firm and secure."* This anchor provides us with an unbreakable spiritual lifeline. This verse not only tells us how our souls are anchored, it tells us where our souls are anchored. J.B. Phillips translates Hebrews 6:19 in this way. *"This hope we hold as the utterly reliable anchor for our souls fixed in the innermost shrine of Heaven, where Jesus has already entered on our behalf."* Our souls are anchored in heaven itself; in the place of finality and of eternity with God. This is the only sense in which the figure of the anchor is used in the Bible.

Fanny J. Crosby's final hymn depicted this perfectly. Crosby was one of the most well-known and dearly loved hymn writers who ever lived. During her lifetime, she wrote over 2000 hymns that were translated into many languages.

She died on the morning of February 12, 1914. Just hours before her death, she wrote the words for her last hymn, and they stand as her final testimony.

> In the morn of Zion's glory
> When the clouds have rolled away,
> And my hope has dropped its anchor
> In the vail of perfect day;
>
> When with all the pure and holy
> I shall strike my harp anew,
> With a Pow'r no arm can sever,
> Love will hold me fast and true.

*"Jesus Christ is the same yesterday and today and forever."* There is an anchor that holds! There is a firm foundation, and it is ours in Jesus. There is eternal and perpetual freshness in Him. He meets us every day with new surprises of His Love and Grace. Sometimes they come to us like a flash of lightning or with the crash of thunder. Sometimes they come with the quietness of the early morning dew.

He is not changing! He is not dying!! He is alive forevermore!!! In Revelation 22:13 we read these words. *"I am the Alpha and the Omega, the First and the Last, the Beginning and the End."* He is always starting something new. He always completes what He has begun. He cannot be defeated. He cannot be destroyed. He can never be weary. His Love is unfailing. He is always with us.

This is a great song of beauty and of encouragement that brightens our way, that confirms our hope and that strengthens our faith. I invite you to take the time to listen carefully to the music that rings out with beauty and joy and affirmation as we prayerfully consider our text and Jesus Christ, the same yesterday and today and forever.

Not long ago I read of two men who were walking down a busy street together. When a church carillon began to play, one commented to the other on how beautiful the music was. The second man, being hard of hearing said, "What's that you say?" The first man replied, "The music. It is lovely!" The second man replied, "I can't understand you." The first man said, "I am just enjoying the beauty of the music." To which the second man replied, "It's no use. I can't under-stand you until that dad-gum noise quiets down!" He was so familiar with the carillon that he no longer heard the music. Don't let your familiarity with this verse drown out the music!

Often, in order to gain a better understanding, a new appreciation, in order to go deeper, we need to get technical. First, let us consider the exclusive and particular title employed; Jesus Christ. Christ was originally a title but later became a part of the name Jesus Christ. The writer of Hebrews only links these two names together three times in the span of 13 chapters. He uses it when he speaks of Jesus Christ as the One through Whom our sanctification is accomplished.

*"We have been made holy through the sacrifice of the body of Jesus Christ once for all"* (Hebrews 10:10). In Hebrews 13:20-21, he speaks of Jesus Christ as the One through Whom God makes us perfect to do His will. *"Now may the God of peace . . . equip you with everything good for doing his will,*

*and may he work in us what is pleasing to him, through Jesus Christ, to whom be glory for ever and ever. Amen."* The writer uses this title a third time when He is referring to Jesus as The Unchanging One as illustrated in Hebrews 13:8, our lesson's text. *"Jesus Christ is the same yesterday and today and forever."* What is he saying to us when he uses this name?

We don't know who wrote the Book of Hebrews, but the simple name of Jesus is often used. Jesus was a Hebrew name. In fact, it was the Greek form of the old Hebrew name, Joshua. There were hundreds of boys in Galilee and Judea who bore that name. It was a name like the name "James" is today. In our family we have James Weldon, James Mark, James Russell and James Ryan. That was the kind of name that "Jesus" was. It was a common name. It was a name that pointed to His humanity, to His oneness with us, to the reality of God with us.

Clearly the writer was not referring here to just another Jesus, for there is this other name; Christ. It is a Messianic name that indicates His work, His assigned duty and His mission. Let's look at the ways this writer of *Hebrews* introduced Him by reading Hebrews 1:1-4.

*"In the past God spoke to our ancestors through the prophets at many times and in various ways, but in these last days he has spoken to us by his Son, whom he appointed heir of all things, and through whom also he made the universe. The Son is the radiance of God's glory and the exact representation of his being, sustaining all things by his powerful word. After he had provided purification for sins, he sat down at the right hand of the Majesty in heaven. So he became as much superior to the angels as the name he has inherited is superior to theirs."*

These two names, Jesus Christ, as they are joined here establish His identity as the Son of God, veiled in human flesh.

Jesus Christ, the same yesterday. Let us turn our attention to yesterday, and we will consider His yesterday that was lived out on this earth. First, we must realize that His teachings did not widely appeal to men. It is true that there were parts of it concerning God's ultimate purposes in this world that appealed to them. However, His call to purity and to obedience aroused rebellion in them, and it still does today.

Yet multitudes were drawn to Him, not by what He taught, but by what He was. He Himself appealed to humanity in its need. When He came into their midst he made hypocrisy impossible. People could not hide themselves. They could not pretend to be something they were not. They could not help taking off their masks. They were compelled to do so, because He saw them, and He knew them for who they really were.

Their sin was laid bare, and He never excused it. He never suggested that it was some necessary part of a process by which God was moving them to something higher. He never suggested that it was incurable. Sometimes we speak of "necessary evils", or of "hopeless cases". Jesus would have seen such expressions as absurd contradictions. To Him, no evil was ever necessary, and no case was ever hopeless. Over and over again lives were redeemed as He confronted them, for in being brought face to face with Him they came face to face with themselves.

He dealt with humanities' sorrow. He never ignored it. It was a great reality to Him. He was *"a man of sorrows, and acquainted with grief"* (Isaiah 53:3). It has been said that the sorrows of earth are most keenly felt in heaven. The sorrows He encountered deeply wounded

His heart. I think of my friend who sobbed out in sorrow, "Lord, where were You?" And He answered her, "I was there, and I cried too." How-ever, He never gave sorrow the final word. He never yielded to it. He never gave in to despair. He mastered it. He took sorrow and turned it to joy!

As we look back to the days of His flesh, we see that He was constantly surprising those about Him. I love something Dr. Morgan wrote. He wrote that Jesus trained his disciples by surprise after surprise after surprise.

Those men had followed Him, and they thought they knew Him. Then He would confound them by something He said or did. He would stop them in their tracks until they discovered what He meant, or the value of what He was doing. Now they knew Him! Now they understood Him; but then they would be confronted by yet another wonder. Who was this man?

Dr. Morgan wrote, "He was so human that they called Him Jesus of Nazareth. Yet out of that human personality there were always breaking lights and glories and powers and revelations and surprises." How are we to account for this?

We account for it because of the longer yesterday, the yesterday that includes all the infinite mysteries of the far-flung splendors of the ages about which we can only dream and about which we know nothing. In the beginning was the Word, John 1:1, and when it was revealed in human form and tabernacled among us, walking human pathways, and mixing among human beings, then lights gleamed and glories flashed surprising the hearts of those who were about Him. Jesus Christ yesterday!

What of Jesus Christ today? Our text speaks of His being the same, but there is a difference. We cannot see Him. He is gone out of sight. He said, *"In a little while you will see me no more, and then after a little while you will see me"* (John 16:16). His promise was no reference to His second coming. He was referring to something that would be immediate.

These men, Peter, James, John, Philip, Thomas and Jude, these men heard Him talk in the Upper Room. Then they lost Him. He passed out of their sight. But when Pentecost came, although they could not see Him with their eyes they saw Him as they had never seen Him before. He had not changed but their perception of Him had changed.

Jesus said to them, *"But very truly I tell you, it is for your good that I am going away"* (John 16:7). Why was it for their good? Because while He was with them He was limited by His flesh. Passing out of sight He would come again through the Holy Spirit to be the inner companion of all who put their trust in Him. He would be able to come into the consciousness of every person who opened their life to Him. It would be a nearer association, but one that cannot be seen by the physical eye.

In John 1:18 we read that "no one has seen God at any time," but at the same time it is true that no one has seen man at any time. You have never seen me, and I have never seen you. What we see are these earth suits that we live in. Jesus was saying to these men that by living in a physical body He was shut outside of them. However, He would go away and then come back in order to take up living His Life right in their innermost spirit. He would show Himself to them by His Spirit, and they would know Him as they never could while He remained outside of them.

In John 17:25-26, we read the following words that make up part of what is known as Jesus' High Priestly Prayer. It was prayed immediately before He was arrested. *"Righteous Father, though the world does not know you, I know you, and they know that you have sent me. I have made you known to them, and will continue to make you known in order that the love you have for me may be in them and that I myself may be in them."*

Today, we can have a closer fellowship with Him than we do with our dearest friend. With Jesus, we can have full and complete and deeply satisfying spiritual fellowship. We know Him through the letters He has written to us. We know Him through dear ones who have allowed Him to transform their thoughts and their lives in ways that reveal Jesus to us. We know Him through our own experiences with Him.

Jesus Christ, the same, yesterday and today. He knows us completely. He still deals with our sins. He still carries our sorrows. He still calls us to come to Him, and He will give us rest. He still surprises us in ways that move us forward in our knowledge and understanding of Him.

Furthermore, He is the same forever. A better translation would be, "He is the same to the ages." Behind us lie the ages. Before us lie the ages. The one who fashions the ages, who shapes and forms the ages, who determines their nature, who controls their forces, who limits their duration, is alive in human history and in human lives and in our lives! Forever is vast. To the ages cannot be fathomed, but they will never be boring or limiting or monotonous.

The Unchanging One is with us. This is one of the greatest blessings of the Christian life. He is the firm foundation on which a life of the beauty of Christ can be built and revealed. He is the center of all that is permanent and immoveable in our lives. He is the spring of all that is perpetually fresh. His mercies are new every morning. He meets us every day, offering us Himself!

How do you accept Him into Your today? There is no better way than through praise and thanksgiving in all things. Bring Him into your life, your circumstances, your joys and your heartbreaks, your gladness and your fears. Bring Him in by claiming His promises through genuine thanksgiving. Confusion will be replaced by steadfast hope. Doubt and fear will be replaced by faith and quiet confidence. The beauty of Jesus will be seen in you, for the One who never changes is with you, and His Love will hold you fast and true.

## To Your Name Be the Glory

Not to us, O Lord;
Not to us, O Lord,
but to Your Name be the glory;
to Your Name be the glory.
To Your name be the glory.
Because of your Love and Faithfulness.

## *Think on These Things*

Can you share one or two ways in which you are newly aware of change taking place in your life?

Can you describe how this is stressful?

Have you considered what you can seek beyond permanence?

How are you pursuing this?

List some of the ways in which we experience Jesus as the one who never changes.

Can you bear witness to what that contributes to your life?

I think you will enjoy reading and thinking about Hebrews Chapter 3.

# The Prayer for Spiritual Life

How to know Jesus Christ as your personal Lord and Savior by being born spiritually into the family of God:

- God loves you, and He created you to have a personal relationship with Him. (Romans 5:8-11).

- Sin separates us from God and His love. We are all born of the seed of Adam, separated from the Life of God by Adam's sin. We are not sinners because we sin. We sin because we are born sinners. (Romans 5:15-18).

- Through Jesus' death and resurrection, Jesus paid the debt that was owed for the sins of mankind. Jesus made it possible to offer forgiveness of sin and a spiritual birth into the family of God. (Romans 6:23; John 14:6; John 3:16-17).

- Jesus left this world and returned to His Father in heaven. Jesus asked God to send the Holy Spirit to be with us and to live in us. God gives us His Life, and makes of us a new creation. Old things pass away and all things become new. (Galatians 5:22; John 14:16-17; 2 Corinthians 5:17).

- You may use the following prayer to express your decision to receive Jesus Christ as your Lord and Savior, and your desire to be born into the family of God:

"Dear God, You have told me in Your Word that I was born a sinner, separated from the Life of God. I believe that Jesus Christ lived and died and rose again so that I can be born spiritually into Your family. I believe that Jesus

Christ asked You to send the Holy Spirit to come live in me and through me, to make me a new creation. I believe that You have given me eternal life, and the opportunity to grow into spiritual maturity. I receive it all now, a brand-new beginning, in the name of Jesus Christ and with thanksgiving and praise. Amen."

\* \* \*

*"Very truly I tell you, whoever hears my word and believes him who sent me has eternal life and will not be judged but has crossed over from death to life"* (John 5:24).

*"The Lord is patient with you, not wanting anyone to perish but everyone to come to repentance"* (2 Peter 3:9).

# Acknowledgments

Praise and honor be to our God, who daily reveals the truth of His Word to those who diligently seek Him.

It is with deep gratitude that I express my appreciation to the following for their contributions:

To Irma Rodriguez. Irma worked for my longtime friend, Mary Jo Scheideman. For many years, she prepared the meeting place for our Bible study every Thursday morning. Coffee and treats would be ready. Chairs would be in place, and Irma would be standing by the front door to welcome us. We miss you, Irma!

To my husband, James Jackson. Throughout the writing of this book he has been battling health problems, but he has been a constant encouragement to me!

To Kathleen Fritsche. She started us down the road to publication. Her work was thoroughly professional. She met every deadline. She was a delight to work with!

To our Thursday Bible Study. Thank you for your faithful prayers, your words of encouragement, and your amazing support. I am forever grateful!

Sincere thanks to Lynn Jackson Talley, who completed the revisions and designed the cover.

# Notes

Lesson 1: Why Did Jesus Come?, Part 1
Adapted from the work of G. Campbell Morgan, *The Westminster Pulpit*, Vol. I (Westwood, N.J., Fleming H. Revell Co., 1954), pp. 298-311.

Lesson 2: Why Did Jesus Come?, Part 2
Adapted from the work of G. Campbell Morgan, The Westminster Pulpit, Vol. I (Westwood, N.J. Fleming H. Revell Co., 1954), pp. 312-325.

Lewis Sperry Chafer, d.d., Litt.D., *Systematic Theology1, Vol. II* (Dallas Seminary Press, 1947), pp. 33-111.

Lesson 3: Why Did Jesus Come?, Part 3
Adapted from the work of G. Campbell Morgan, *The Westminster Pulpit, Vol. I* (Westwood, N.J. Fleming H. Revell Co., 1954), pp. 326-338.

Lesson 4: Finding New Beginnings
Adapted from the work of G. Campbell Morgan, *The Westminster Pulpit, Vol. 9* (Westwood, N.J., Fleming H. Revell Co., 1954), pp. 78-91.

Henri J.M. Nouwen, Here and Now: *Living in the Spirit*, (Crossroad Publishing Co., 1994), pp. 16-17.

Lesson 5: Have You Decided to Follow Jesus?
Adapted from the work of G. Campbell Morgan, *The Westminster Pulpit, Vol. IV* (Westwood, N.J., Fleming H. Revell Co., 1954), pp. 162-175.

Henri J.M. Nouwen, *Bread for the Journey*, (Harper, San Francisco, 1997) January 11.

Lesson 6: What is Our Part in the Christian Life? What is God's Part? Adapted from the work of G. Campbell Morgan, *The Westminster Pulpit, Vol. I* (Westwood, N.J., Fleming H. Revell Co., 1954), pp. 46-57.

Hannah Whitall Smith, *The Christian's Secret of a Happy Life*, (Random House Publishing Group, 1986).

Lesson 7: Secret Things and Revealed Things
Adapted from the work of G. Campbell Morgan, *The Westminster Pulpit, Vol. III* (Westwood, N.J., Fleming H. Revell Co., 1954), pp. 22-34.

Andrew Murray, *The Inner Life*, (Zondervan Publishing Co., 1980).

Lesson 8: What is the Secret of Jehovah?
Adapted from the work of G. Campbell Morgan, *The Westminster Pulpit, Vol. IV* (Westwood, N.J., Fleming H. Revell Co., 1954), pp. 216-228.

Lesson 9: Jubilation in Desolation
Adapted from the work of G. Campbell Morgan, *The Westminster Pulpit, Vol. VI* (Westwood, N.J., Fleming H. Revell Co., 1954), pp. 140-153.

Lesson 10: He Never Changes
Adapted from the work of G. Campbell Morgan, *The Westminster Pulpit, Vol. IX* (Westwood, N.J., Fleming H. Revell Co., 1954), pp. 65-77.

Miscellaneous Bibliography

Dr. J. Vernon McGee, *Through the Bible with J. Vernon McGee* (Thomas Nelson, Inc., 1981).

John F. Walvoord, Roy B. Zuck, *The Bible Knowledge Commentary: Old Testament and New Testament* (2 Volume Set), (David C. Cook Publishing Company, 2002).

Made in the USA
Coppell, TX
21 January 2026

69150297R00115